UTTOXETER TO MACCLESFIELD

via Leek

Vic Mitchell

MP Middleton Press

Front cover: Approaching Leek Brook Junction on the line from Stoke-on-Trent, on 29th October 1966, is class 2MT 2-6-2T no. 41204. (Colour-Rail.com)

Back cover: Route diagram of 1947. (Railway Clearing House)

Published May 2017

ISBN 978 1 910356 05 0

Production Editor Deborah Esher
Typesetting & design Cassandra Morgan
Cover design Matthew Esher

Published by
>   *Middleton Press*
>   *Easebourne Lane*
>   *Midhurst*
>   *West Sussex*
>   *GU29 9AZ*
Tel: 01730 813169
Email: info@middletonpress.co.uk
www.middletonpress.co.uk

Printed and bound by CPI Group (UK) Ltd, Croydon, CR0 4YY

INDEX

ACKNOWLEDGEMENTS

I am very grateful for the assistance received from many of those mentioned in the credits, also from A.J.Castledine, G.Croughton, G.Gartside, J.Horne, C.M.Howard, C.Knight, N.Langridge, B.Lewis, Mr D. and Dr S. Salter, K.Smith and T.Walsh. Thanks also go to the Churnet Valley Railway, Leek & Rudyard Railway, and in particular my always supportive family.

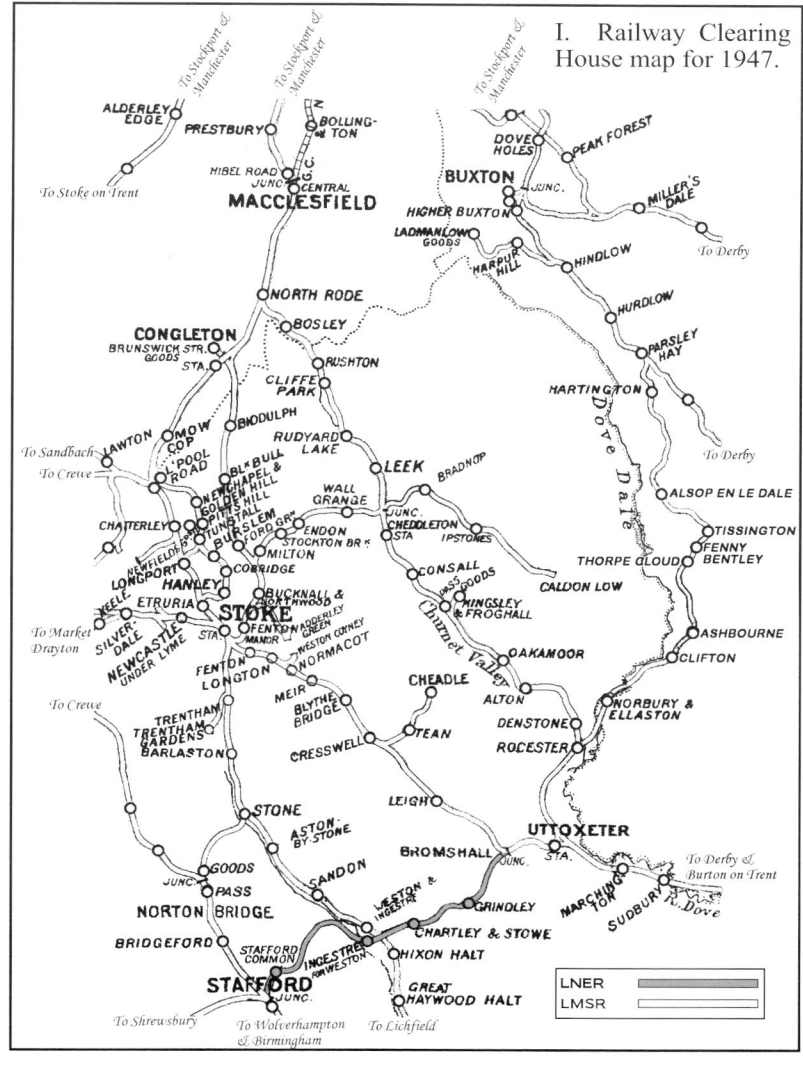

I. Railway Clearing House map for 1947.

GEOGRAPHICAL SETTING

The district is at the southern end of the Pennine Hills and the River Dove flows south in a deep valley to reach Uttoxeter. Here it turns east and eventually drains into the River Trent, north of Burton-on-Trent.

Joining the Dove near Rocester is the River Churnet, which flows east. It first runs south around the market town of Leek. Also rising north of the town is the River Dane, which flows north, close to our route between Rushton and Bosley.

Close to the line south of Leek is the Caldon Canal, which appears on later maps. It joins the Trent & Mersey Canal in Stoke-on-Trent, as does the Macclesfield Canal, which is close to our route from Bosley northwards.

The geology contains minerals that have been of great value. Their locations are detailed in the captions; they include limestone, sandstone, copper and sand. Locally, copper was initially mined at Ecton, in the Manifold Valley; see picture 90 in *Branch Line from Leek*. The ore was later transported great distances to the works in the Churnet Valley, which were powered by the river.

The line was built largely in Staffordshire; the section from Rushton northwards was created in Cheshire.

The maps are to the scale of 25ins to 1 mile with north at the top, unless otherwise indicated.

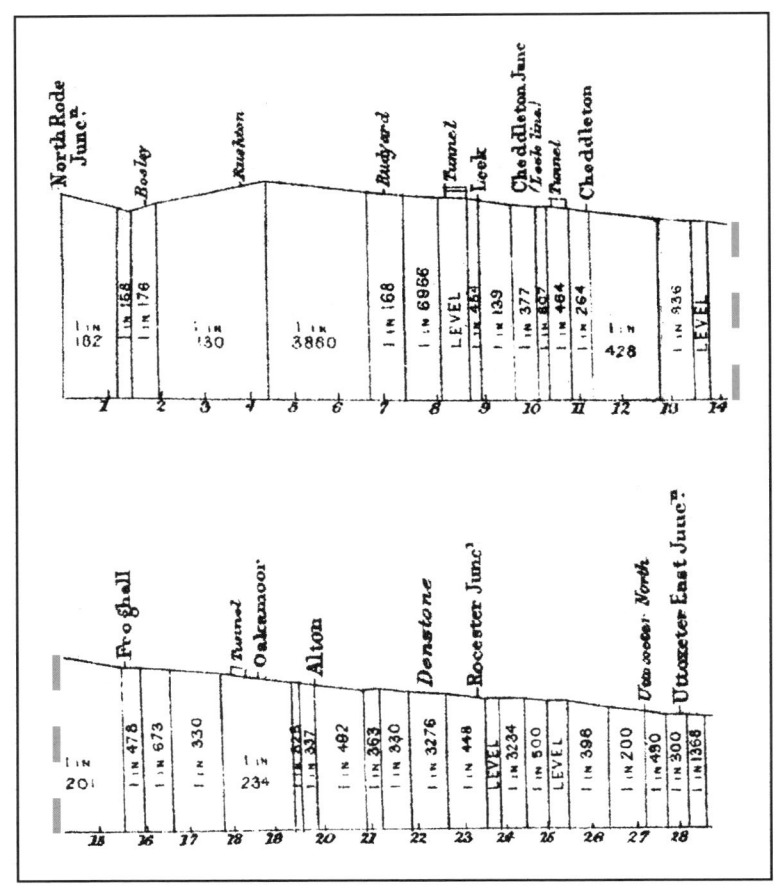

HISTORICAL BACKGROUND

The 1839 Birmingham & Derby Junction Railway was linked to Stoke-on-Trent by the North Staffordshire Railway in 1848 - west of Uttoxeter on 7th August 1848 and east thereof on 11th September 1848. The Act was dated 28th June 1846.

A line ran north from Burton-on-Trent and a direct east-west link to Uttoxeter was added by October 1849.

The NSR ran north from Uttoxeter from 1st August 1849, reaching Macclesfield on 1st September of that year. The route westwards from Leek was in use from 1867 until 1956, for passengers.

The NSR became a constituent of the London Midland & Scottish Railway, when the grouping took place in 1923. The line north of Burton lost its local trains on 1st January 1949 and all services in 1968. Freight closures are given in the captions.

Upon nationalisation in 1948, the LMSR was largely allocated to the London Midland Region of British Railways, while most of the LNER entered the Eastern Region. Passenger service was withdrawn between Leek and Macclesfield on 7th November 1960 and between Uttoxeter and Leek on 4th January 1965. Leek to Waterhouses services had ceased in 1935, but those from Leek to Stoke-on-Trent lasted until 1956.

Local goods closure dates are shown in the captions. The mineral lines west, east and south of Leek Brook Junction were retained to link Stoke-on-Trent with Caldon Low and Oakamoor. They were mostly closed by 1988-89, but largely remained in place to eventually serve new private railway companies. These included the North Staffordshire Railway (1978) Ltd, the Churnet Valley Railway since 1992 and Moorland & City Railways from 2009. The route to Stoke-on-Trent from Leek Brook was also acquired by M&CR. There were some directors on the boards of both the latter and the CVR.

PASSENGER SERVICES

The table gives sample figures for trains running on at least five days per week.

	Uttoxeter-Leek		Leek-Macclesfield	
	Weekdays	Sundays	Weekdays	Sundays
1850	4	2	4	2
1860	5	2	4	2
1890	4	1	4	1
1924	7	4	6	4
1959	5	2	5	2
1964	3	0	-	-

Most of the trains shown above called at all stations. In the early years, there were a few trains which were extended to Derby and/or Manchester, on weekdays. In later years, there were some holiday-time services that ran to and from East Coast resorts, mainly on Saturdays and often from Manchester.

In the 1890s, there were one or two London-Manchester trains via Stoke and Leek. There were some that started at Stoke, notably on Saturday evenings. Trains serving the pleasure locations on the routes grew in number during the 1920s, notably during Summer weekends.

Cruise trains were a feature of the 1930s, these running slowly near the lakes, rivers and many scenic attractions. The 1950s brought several holiday trains each week in the Summers along the route, between Manchester and Lowestoft.

February 1890

CREWE, MACCLESFIELD, LEEK, UTTOXETER, BURTON, and DERBY.—N.S.

Offices—Stoke-upon-Trent. Sec., Percy Morris. Res. Eng., G. J. Crosbie Dawson.

Station															Sundays.			
246 Manchester (Londn Rd.) dp	....	....		7 0	10 0	....		1145	....	3 5	3 15	4 20	....	6 20	mrn	mrn	4 30	aft
245 Liverpool (Lime St.) .. "	....	2 35		7 10	9 45	....		12 0	....	3 5	4 5	5 20	....	7 0	....	2 0	4 0	....
Chester 224 .... "	....	2b25		6 55	1010	....		1150	....	2 20	4 20	5 25	....	7 30	....	2 25	4 20	....
Crewe .... dep	....	7 15	Arrives at Horninglow, Burton, and Derby (Friargate), via Egginton and Great Northern Line.	8 35	1050	....	Wednesdays and Saturdays.	1 35	....	4 20	4 59	6 25	Runs via Stoke.	8 40	a Stops to set down from Stations beyond Crewe on informing the Guard at Stoke.	8 5	5 22	....
Radway Green	....	7 25		8 45	11 0	....		exp	....	....	5 14	exp		8 50		8 15	5 32	....
Alsager (Rode Heath) [254	....	7 31		8 50	11 5	....		1 47	....	4 32	5 19	6 38		8 55		8 20	5 37	....
Harecastle (Kidsgrv) 253,	....	7 40		8 56	1111	1218		1 53	....	4 38	5 25	6 45		9 1		8 28	5 43	9 2
Chatterley	....	7 45		9 1	....	1225		....	....	f	5 31	....		9 6		8 33	5 49	9 7
Longport, for Wolstanton	....	7 50		9 6	1119	1231		2 0	....	f	5 37	6 51		9 11		8 38	5 54	9 12
Etruria, for Basford	6 29	7 54		9 12	1125	1237		2 6	4 19	f	5 43	6 56		9 15		8 44	6 0	9 18
Stoke 251, and below ... a	6 32	8 1		9 17	1130	1242		2 10	4 22	4 48	5 47	7 0		9 20		8 48	6 3	9 22
To M. Drayton, p. 251 ... dep	6 33	8 10		9 25	1133	1253		2 13	4 23	4 51	5 58	7 3		9 24		9 5	6 5	9 25
Fenton	6 37	....		9 29	....	1257		....	4 27	....	6 2	....		9 29		9 11	6 10	9 31
Longton	6 40	8 18		9 32	1141	1 0		2 20	4 30	4 57	6 5	7 10		9 34		9 15	6 13	9 35
Normacot	....	....		9 35	....	1 3		....	4 33	....	6 9	....		9 38		9 18	6 16	
Blyth Bridge	6 46	8 26		d Stops to set down from Stas. North of Crewe & Stockport on informing Guard at Stoke; & by signal to take up for Burton, Derby, & beyond.	1149	....		....	4 38	a	6 14	d		9 45		9 23	6 22	b Leaves at 2 4 mrn. on Mondays. c Via Derby, re-booking there. e Saturdays only. g Except Saturdays.
Cresswell	6 51	8 31			1154	....		....	4 43	a	6 19	dk		9 51		9 28	6 27	
Leigh	6 58	8 39			12 1	....		....	4 50	a		d		9 59		9 35	6 34	
Uttoxeter 168, 253 ...... arr	7 8	8 49			1211	....		2 43	5 0	5 18	f Passengers for these Stations change at Harecastle, arriving at Chatterley 4 50, Longport 4 56, and Etruria 5 3 aft.	7 34		1010		9 45	6 44	
249 Manchester (Londn Rd.) L.&N.W. dep	....	6 15			9 45	....	12 0	....		2 45		5 30	7 30	j Stops by signal to take up 1st class Passengers for London. k Stops on Saturdays to set down Local Passengers.		8 0	....	
326 M. S. & L. "	....	....			9 5	....	1050	....		1e30		4g20	6 50			7 0	....	
248 Buxton (via Middlewd) "	....	....			9h0	h	1050	....		1h20		3l35	5 15			....	....	
Mls Macclesfield Hibel Rd.	....	7 15			1022	....	1247	....	h Via Stockport, L. & N. W. l Stops to set down return ticket holders to Leek and beyond, on informing the Guard at Leek.	3 30		6 10	8 3			9 0	....	
¼ Central	....	7 17			1024	....	1249	....		3 32		6 12	8 6			9 2	....	
5 North Rode Junction	....	7 27			1035	....	1259	....		3 42		6 22	....			9 12	....	
6¼ Bosley	....	7 32			1040	....	1 4	....		3 47		6 27	....			9 17	....	
8¾ Rushton	....	7 38			1046	....	1 10	....		3 53		6 32	....			9 23	....	
11¼ Rudyard	....	7 46			1053	....	1 18	....		4 1		6 39	....			9 31	....	
13¾ Leek 251	....	7 52			1058	....	1 24	....		4 7		6 45	....			9 37	....	
16¼ Cheddleton	....	7 58			11 3	....	1 30	....		4 14		6 51	....			9 45	....	
20¼ Froghall	....	8 7			1112	....	1 39	....		4 24		7 0	....			9 54	....	
23¼ Oakamoor	....	8 14			1118	....	1 46	....		4 31		7 7	....			10 1	....	
24¾ Alton	....	8 20			1122	....	1 51	....		4 36		7 13	....			10 7	....	
27¼ Denstone Crossing	....	8 26			Wd	....	Sig.	....		4 43		i	....			1014	....	
28¾ Rocester Junction 253	7 1	8 31	9 20		1130	....	2 1	2 24		4 47		7 22	....		9 41	1019	6 30	
32¾ Uttoxeter 168, 253 ..arr	7 10	8 39	9 28		1138	....	2 10	2 32		4 55		7 30	1010		9 50	1027	6 39	
Uttoxeter .... dep	7 40	8 54	9 42		1215	....		2 46		5 21		7 38	....		l Via Stockport on Saturdays.	1034	6 49	
Marchington	....	9 1	9 47		....	....	....	....		5 27		....	....			1040	6 56	
Sudbury	7 50	9 7	9 51		1225	....	....	j		5 33		7 52	....			1048	7 5	
Tutbury	8 0	9 16	9 58		1234	....	....	3 0		5 41		8 4	....			1056	7 17	
Tutbury .... dep	8 17	9 20	....		1238	....	....	3 5		5 46		8 8	....			11 0	7 24	
Horninglow	8 26	9 30	1017		1249	....	....	3 15		5 56		8 18	....			1110	7 35	
Burton 211, 274, 277, 282 ar	8 30	9 33	1020		1253	....	....	3 18		5 59		8 21	....			1118	7 39	
London (Euston) 199 ..arr	1 0	8 10	3 10		5 5	....	....	7 0		9 45		....	....			....	....	
Egginton Junction 169	8 7	9 24	10 7		1241	....	....	....		5 48		8 14	....			11 4	7 27	
Nottingham 169 ......arr	9 26	1112	1112		2 1	....	....	4 44		7 4		9 45	....			2c16	1011	
157 London (King's Cross) .. "	1 0	1 55	1 55		5 20	....	....	7 55		9 45		2 10	....			7c50	2 50	
Derby 265, 261, 255, 268, 279	8 23	9 40	1023		1257	....	....	3 20		6 5		8 30	....			1120	7 45	
Nottingham 255 ......arr	9 23	1050	1056		2 0	....	....	4 13		6 57		9 27	....			2 27	9 10	
Leicester 265 .... "	9 26	1133	1219		1 55	....	....	4 29		7 28		1044	....			2 42	9 45	
265 London (St. Pancras) .. "	1150	2 35	2 35		4 15	....	....	7 15		9 40		4 15	....			5 0	4 15	

For other Trains, see below.

July 1924

MACCLESFIELD, LEEK, and UTTOXETER.—L. M. & S.

Up. — Week Days.

Miles from Macclesfield (Hibel Road.)	London Road Station,	mrn	mrn	mrn	mrn	mrn	mrn W		aft S	aft	aft S	aft W		aft	aft S	aft S	aft E	aft		aft S	aft S			
	418 Manchester ...dep.	....	5 40	6 55	7 40	9 20	....	....	....	12 20	1 d 5	....	....	2 45	....	3 55	4 35	5 25	....	....	9 15	....	....	....
	421 Buxton ..... "	....	....	....	....	8 27	....	....	....	11e25	....	....	....	1b20	....	....	3 15	4a25	....	....	7 35	....	....	....
	418 Stockport ..... "	....	5 55	7 5	8 5	9 30	....	....	....	12 30	1 20	....	....	2 55	....	4 5	4 45	5 37	....	....	9 25	....	....	....
	Macclesfield (H. Rd.) dep.	....	6 38	7 45	8 50	10 5	....	....	....	1 2	2 13	....	....	3 35	....	5 0	5 28	6 12	....	....	1015	....	....	....
	421 Buxton ......dep.	....	....	....	7 40	8 40	....	....	....	10s35	....	....	....	12s35	....	....	....	4a25	....	....	9 0	....	....	....
	824 Middlewood ... "	....	....	....	8 20	9 36	....	....	....	11 46	....	....	....	1n49	....	....	....	5e3	....	....	7 43	....	....	....
¼	Macclesfield (Central) ..	....	6 42	....	8 53	10 7	....	....	....	1 4	....	....	....	3 37	....	5 2	5 30	6 15	....	....	1017	....	....	....
5	North Rode	....	6 52	8B5	9 4	10 17	....	....	....	1 14	2 23	....	....	3 47	....	5 12	5 40	6 26	....	....	1027	....	....	....
6¼	Bosley	....	6 57	8 10	9 10	10 22	....	....	....	1 19	2 28	....	....	3 52	....	5 17	5 45	6 31	....	....	1032	....	....	....
8¾	Rushton	....	7 3	8 15	9 16	10 27	....	....	....	1 25	2 33	....	....	3 57	....	5 25	5 50	6 36	....	....	1037	....	....	....
9¾	Rudyard Lake	....	....	8 18	9 20	10 30	....	....	....	1 28	2 36	....	....	4 0	....	5 28	5 53	6 39	....	....	....	....	....	....
11¼	Rudyard	....	7 11	8 24	9 26	10 36	....	....	....	1 33	2 42	....	....	4 6	....	5 35	5 59	6 45	....	9 0	1045	....	....	....
13¾	Leek 526, 532	....	7 15	8 28	9 30	10 44	1150	....	1245	1 44	2 50	3 20	....	4 14	5 0	5 39	6 9	6 57	....	9 10	1049	....	....	....
16¼	Cheddleton	....	7 26	....	....	10 49	1155	....	1250	1 49	2 55	3 25	....	4 18	5 5	....	6 14	7 2	....	9 15	....	....	....	....
18½	Consall	....	7 31	....	....	10 54	12 0	....	1255	1 54	3 0	3 30	....	4 26	5 10	....	6 19	7 7	....	9 20	....	....	....	....
20¼	Kingsley and Froghall	6 20	7 38	....	....	11 0	12 5	....	1 1	2 0	3 6	3 35	....	4 32	5 15	....	6 25	7 13	....	9 26	....	....	....	....
23¼	Oakamoor	6 26	7 44	....	....	11 6	....	....	1 6	2 6	3 11	....	....	4 38	....	....	6 30	7 18	....	9 31	....	....	....	....
24¾	Alton	6 31	7 49	....	....	11 11	....	....	1 11	2 11	3 16	....	....	4 43	....	....	6 35	7 24	....	9 36	....	....	....	....
27½	Denstone	6 37	7 55	....	....	11 17	....	....	1 17	2 17	3 22	....	....	4 49	....	....	6 41	7 30	....	9 42	....	....	....	....
28¾	Rocester 530 [532	6 40	7 58	....	....	11 20	....	....	1 20	2 20	3 25	....	....	4 52	....	....	6 44	7 33	....	9 45	....	....	....	....
32¾	Uttoxeter 522, 523 arr.	6 49	8 8	....	....	11 30	....	....	1 30	2 30	3 35	....	....	5 2	....	....	6 54	7 46	....	9 55	....	....	....	....
46	522 Burton-on-Trent† ar	7 52	9 27	....	....	12A36	....	....	....	3 17	....	....	....	6 3	....	....	....	8 40	....	10 57	....	....	....	....
52	522 Derby .... "	7 50	9 3	....	....	1 11	....	....	....	3 17	....	....	....	5 45	....	....	....	8 32	....	10 48	....	....	....	....

Up. — Sundays.

Miles	Station	mrn	aft	aft	aft	aft	aft	aft	
	418 Manchester ...dep.	8 10	1 y 0	3 15	....	5 30	6 50	....	....
	421 Buxton ..... "	....	1015	....	....	....	....	....	....
	418 Stockport ..... "	8 28	1 20	3 26	....	5 42	7 0	....	....
	Macclesfield (H. Rd.) dep.	9 15	2 30	4 35	....	6 23	7 50	....	....
	421 Buxton ......dep.	....	....	....	....	....	....	....	....
	824 Middlewood ... "	....	....	....	....	....	....	....	....
¼	Macclesfield (Central) ..	9 17	2 32	4 37	....	....	7 52	8 58	....
5	North Rode	9 27	2 42	4 47	....	6 33	8 2	9 9	....
6¼	Bosley	9 32	2 47	4 52	....	6 38	8 7	9 14	....
8¾	Rushton	9 37	2 52	5 0	....	6 45	8 15	9 19	....
9¾	Rudyard Lake	9 40	2 55	5 3	....	6 48	8 18	9 22	....
11¼	Rudyard	9 46	3 1	5 10	6 0	6 55	8 25	9 28	....
13¾	Leek 526, 532	9 55	3X15	5 14	6 10	6 59	8X38	9 32	....
16¼	Cheddleton	10 0	3 20	....	6 15	....	8 43	....	....
18½	Consall	10 5	3 25	....	6 20	....	8 48	....	....
20¼	Kingsley and Froghall	1011	3 31	....	6 26	....	8 54	....	....
23¼	Oakamoor	1016	3 36	....	6 31	....	8 59	....	....
24¾	Alton	1021	3 41	....	6 36	....	9 4	....	....
27½	Denstone	1027	3 47	....	6 42	....	9 10	....	....
28¾	Rocester 530 [532	1030	3 50	....	6 45	....	9 13	....	....
32¾	Uttoxeter 522, 523 arr.	1040	4 0	....	6 55	....	9 23	....	....
46	522 Burton-on-Trent† ar	1140	....	....	8 0	....	....	....	....
52	522 Derby .... "	1140	....	....	8 0	....	....	....	....

Down. — Week Days.

Miles from Uttoxeter.	Station	mrn	mrn	mrn	mrn	mrn	mrn		aft W	mrn	aft S	aft S		aft E	aft W	aft S	aft S	aft	aft S	aft S	aft	aft	aft S	
	523 Derby ....dep.	....	....	....	....	7 30	9 20	....	....	11 0	12 0	1 35	....	1 35	....	....	....	5 0	....	6 27	7 15	....	....	....
	523 Burton-on-Trent† "	....	....	....	....	7 10	9 12	....	....	10 55	1152	1 30	....	1 30	....	....	....	4 35	....	5 25	7 5	....	....	....
	Uttoxeter ....dep.	5 40	....	One class only.	7 14	8 15	1010	....	....	12 20	1 5	2 15	....	2 50	....	....	....	5 45	....	7 40	8 30	....	....	....
4½	Rocester	5 48	....		7 22	8 23	1020	....	....	12 28	1 13	2 23	....	2 58	....	....	....	5 53	....	7 48	8 38	....	....	....
5¼	Denstone	5 53	....		7 27	8 28	1025	....	....	12 33	1 18	2 28	....	3 3	....	....	....	5 58	....	7 53	8 43	....	....	....
8	Alton	5 59	....		7 33	8 34	1031	....	....	12 39	1 24	2 34	....	3 9	....	....	....	6 4	....	7 59	8 49	....	....	....
9½	Oakamoor	6 4	....		7 38	8 39	1036	....	....	12 44	1 29	2 39	....	3 14	....	....	....	6 9	....	8 4	8 54	....	....	....
12¼	Kingsley and Froghall	6 10	....		7 46	8 45	1042	....	1220	12 50	1 35	2 45	....	3 20	3 45	....	5 30	6 16	....	8 10	9 0	....	....	....
14¼	Consall	....	....		7 52	8 50	1047	....	1225	12 55	1 40	2 50	....	3 25	3 50	....	5 35	6 22	....	8 15	9s5	....	....	....
16½	Cheddleton	....	....		8 0	8 55	1052	....	1230	1 0	1 45	2 55	....	3 30	3 55	....	5 40	6 28	....	8 20	9 10	....	....	....
19	Leek 526, 532	....	7 15	7 32	8 8	9 2	11h7	....	1235	1 10	2m0	3 5	....	3p40	4 5	4 40	5 45	6 38	7 45	8 30	9 15	9 25	1035	....
21	Rudyard	....	7 20	7 41	8 13	9 7	1114	....	....	1 15	2 5	3 10	....	3 45	4 9	4 45	....	6 43	7 50	8 35	....	9 30	1040	....
23	Rudyard Lake	....	....	....	8 19	a	1120	....	....	1 21	2 11	3 16	....	3 51	....	4 51	....	6 49	7 56	8 41	....	9s36	....	....
24	Rushton	....	7 28	7 53	8 23	9 16	1125	....	....	1 25	2 14	3 20	....	3 55	....	4 55	....	6 53	8 0	8 45	....	9 39	1048	....
26¼	Bosley	....	7 33	8 0	8 28	9 21	1132	....	....	1 30	....	3 25	....	4 0	....	5 10	....	6 58	8 5	8 50	....	9 45	1053	....
27¾	North Rode 524	....	7B38	8 10	8 33	9 26	1137	....	....	1 35	....	3 30	....	4 5	....	5 15	....	7 3	8 10	8 55	....	9 51	1058	....
32½	Macclesfield (C.) 825	....	....	8 31	8 44	....	1147	....	....	1 45	....	3 40	....	4 13	....	....	....	7 11	8 20	....	....	10 1	11 8	....
40	825 Middlewood ... arr.	....	....	....	9 19	....	1249	....	....	4o9	....	4 9	....	6 19	....	....	....	7 49	....	....	....	....	....	....
54¾	420 Buxton .... "	....	....	....	10 23	....	2F25	....	....	5t16	....	5 16	....	....	....	....	....	8 43	....	....	....	....	....	....
32¾	Macclesfield (H.R.) 419 ar	....	8 10	8 32	8 45	9 35	1148	....	....	1 46	....	3 41	....	4 17	....	5 23	....	7 15	8 21	9 5	....	10 2	11 9	....
44½	419 Stockport ..... arr.	....	8 43	....	9 23	10 11	1226	....	....	2i20	....	4 23	....	4 56	....	6 8	....	7 53	8 52	9 47	....	10 56	....	....
64¼	420 Buxton .... "	....	1023	....	....	11e35	2F25	....	....	3 45	....	....	....	6 15	....	8 43	....	....	10 6	1132	....	12k10	....	....
50½	419 M'chester (L.R.) "	....	8 56	....	9 38	10 24	1240	....	....	2dg33	....	4 38	....	5d20	....	6d20	....	8 20	9 7	10 5	....	11 10	....	....

Down. — Sundays.

Miles	Station	mrn	mrn	aft	aft	aft	aft		
	523 Derby ....dep.	....	9 50	1 0	....	6 25	....	....	....
	523 Burton-on-Trent† "	....	9 50	....	....	6 15	....	....	....
	Uttoxeter ....dep.	....	1110	2 5	5 20	7 15	....	....	....
4½	Rocester	....	1118	2 13	5 28	7 23	....	....	....
5¼	Denstone	....	1123	2 18	5 33	7 28	....	....	....
8	Alton	....	1129	2 24	5 39	7 34	....	....	....
9½	Oakamoor	....	1134	2 29	5 44	7 39	....	....	....
12¼	Kingsley and Froghall	7 30	1140	2 35	5 50	7 45	....	....	....
14¼	Consall	....	1145	2 40	5 55	7 50	....	....	....
16½	Cheddleton	7 40	1150	2 45	6 0	7 55	....	....	....
19	Leek 526, 532	7 55	12 2	2 50	6 10	8 8	9 30	....	....
21	Rudyard	7 59	12 7	....	6 15	8 13	9 35	....	....
23	Rudyard Lake	....	1213	....	6 21	8 19	9 41	....	....
24	Rushton	8 11	1217	....	6 25	8 23	9 45	....	....
26¼	Bosley	8 18	1222	....	6 30	[illegible]	9 50	....	....
27¾	North Rode 524	8 26	1227	....	6 35	[illegible]	9 55	....	....
32½	Macclesfield (C.) 825	8 42	1238	....	6 45	8 43	....	....	....
40	825 Middlewood ... arr.	....	....	....	....	....	....	....	....
54¾	420 Buxton .... "	....	....	....	....	....	....	....	....
32¾	Macclesfield (H.R.) 419 ar	8 48	1240	....	6 46	8 45	10 3	....	....
44½	419 Stockport ..... arr.	9 21	1 17	....	7 42	9 29	1040	....	....
64¼	420 Buxton .... "	....	3 18	....	....	....	....	....	....
50½	419 M'chester (L.R.) "	9y50	1 45	....	8 8	9 45	1052	....	....

a Leaves at 3 15 aft. on Saturdays.
A Arrives Burton at 12 18 aft. on Sats.
a Stops to take up for Manchester.
b Leaves Buxton at 12 35 aft. on Sats.
B Change at North Rode.
d Mayfield Station.
E or e Except Saturdays.
F Arrives at 1 48 aft. on Saturdays.
g Arrives (Mayfield Station) 2 47 aft. on Saturdays.
h Arrives Leek at 10 57 mrn.
i Arrives at 2 30 aft. on Saturdays.
k Weds., Thurs., and Sats.
m Arrives at 1 50 aft.
n Leaves at 2 33 aft. on Saturdays.
o Arrives at 2 39 aft. on Saturdays.
p Arrives at 3 35 aft.
S or s Saturdays only.
t Arrives at 3 5 aft. on Saturdays.
W Wednesdays only.
X Arrives Leek about 10 mins. earlier.
y Change at Stockport.
† Station Street.

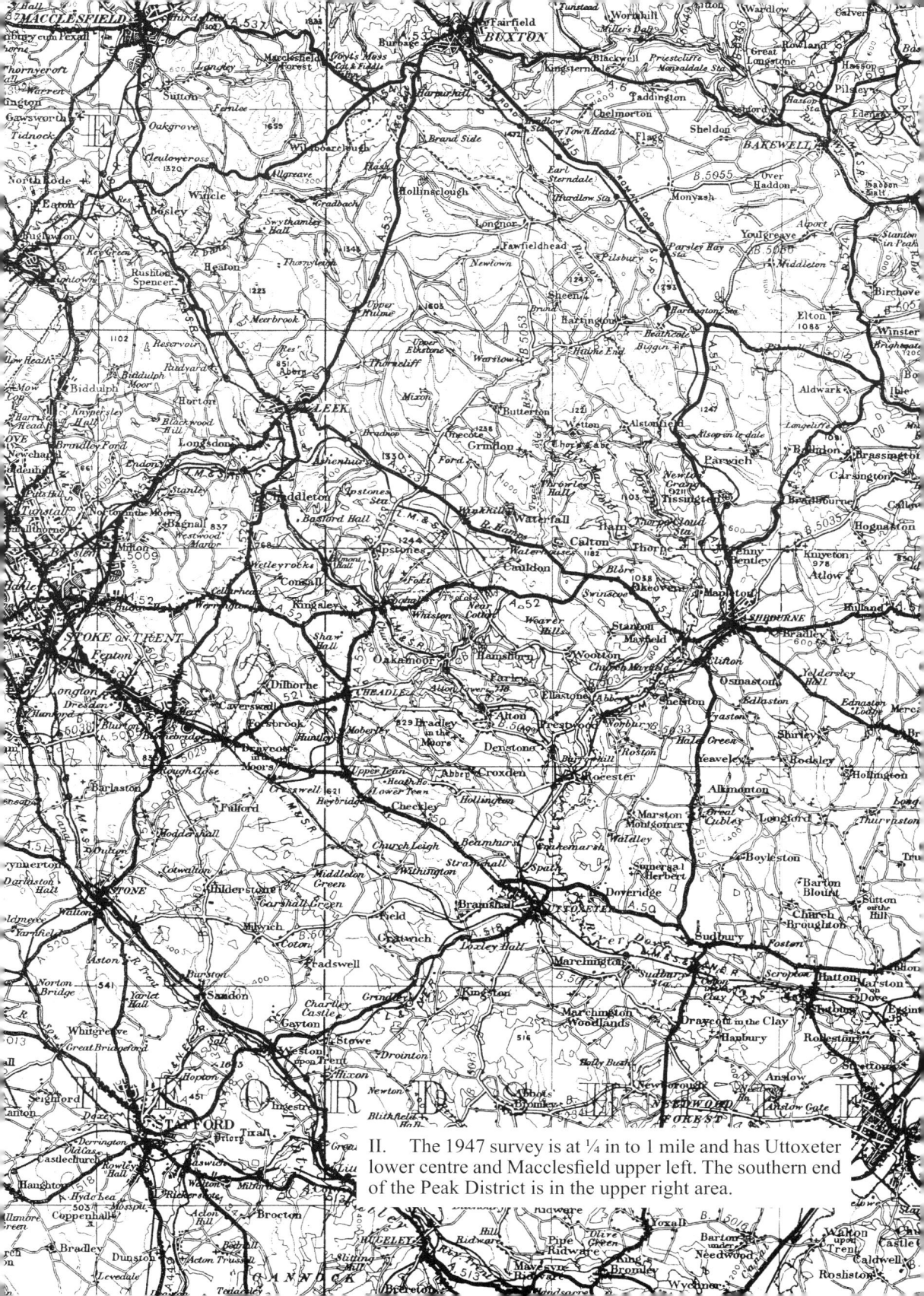

II. The 1947 survey is at ¼ in to 1 mile and has Uttoxeter lower centre and Macclesfield upper left. The southern end of the Peak District is in the upper right area.

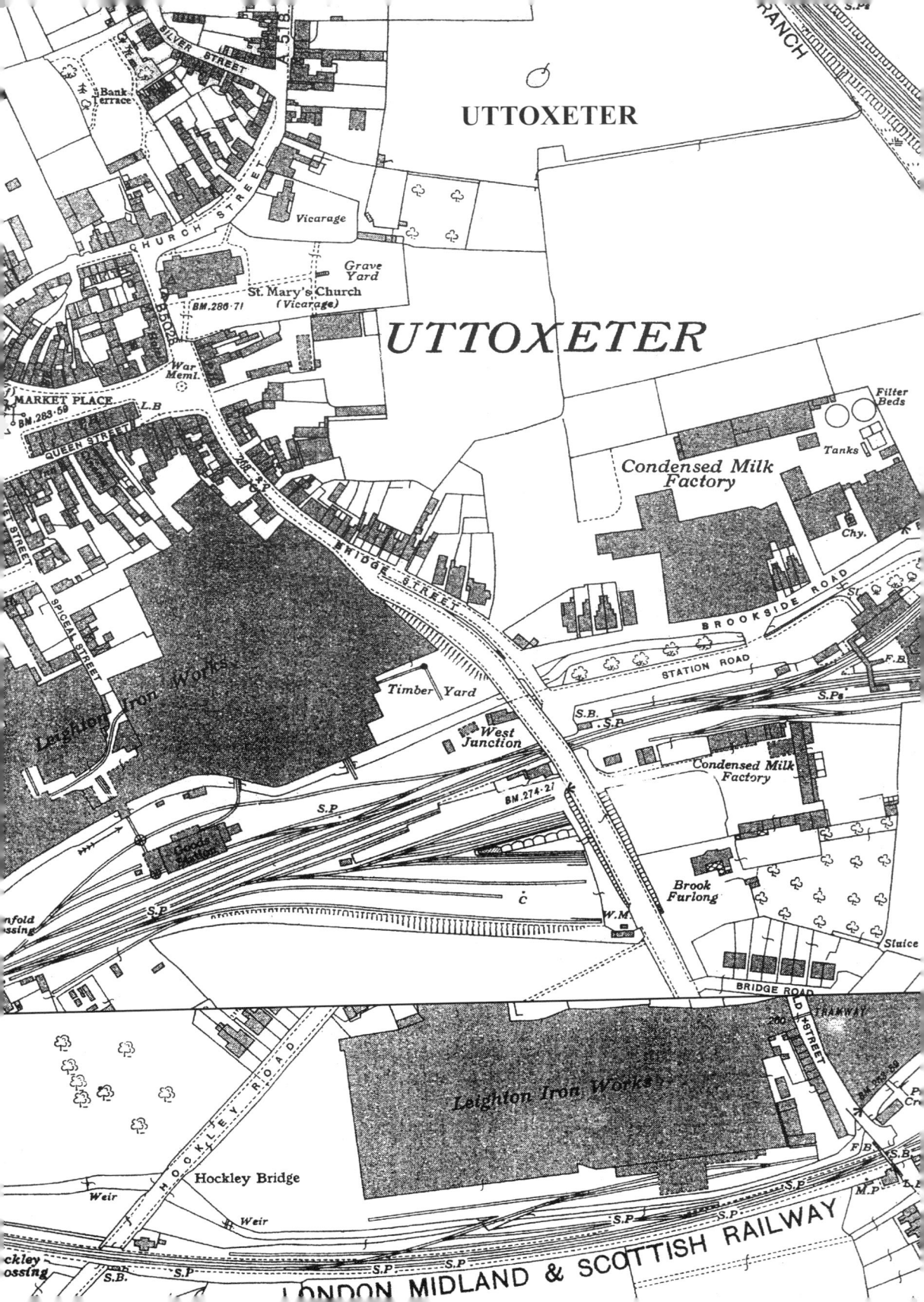

UTTOXETER

UTTOXETER

III. The 1937 edition, at 20ins to 1 mile, has the line from Derby lower right and our route at the top. Inset on the left page is the continuation of the sidings. The iron works became the birthplace of the Bamford family products. The 1881 station is at the join of the pages. The eastern one had been lower right and the northern one is shown in picture 7. The racecourse opened on 3rd May 1907 and is lower right. From Uttoxeter East Junction there was a long siding to Uttoxeter North Shell Mex and BP oil depot, which remained in use, receiving one or two trains per week from Stanlow until 1979.

S.P

S.Ps

S.P

B.M.243·72

Picknal B

Allotment Gardens

Engine Shed

...tion

S.Ps

F.B.

Paddock

S.P

East
Junction

Stands

S.B.

R
a
c
e

C
o
u
r

F.B.

1.   Departing west is NSR 2-4-0 no. 39, while a northbound train waits in the background. Waiting on the left is the shunting horse, about to be coupled to a horse box. (R.M.Casserley coll.)

2.   The date is 22nd May 1948 and the photographer is standing in the dock siding. Macclesfield trains started and terminated in the platforms on the left, which had bidirectional signalling. Having just arrived is LMS class 4P 2-6-4T no. 2665. It will soon receive a BR number. (W.A.Camwell/SLS)

3.   At the other end of these platforms, on the same day, are Stanier locomotives. On the left is a class 4MT 2-6-4T and on the right is a class 3MT 2-6-2T, both devoid of numbers. Common destinations for trains from these platforms were Buxton and Ashbourne. The trains will soon pass North Box, which had 29 levers and was in use from September 1875 until 30th January 1966. (W.A.Camwell/SLS)

4.   The ex-NSR engine shed was photographed on 27th April 1963, with 2-6-4T no. 42224, on the left, and 2-6-0 no. 42826, on the right. The shed code was 5F from 1948 until it closed in 1964. (R.Humm coll.)

5.   It is 9th May 1970 and the track has been lifted from platforms 3 and 4. At the dock, the creamery has a tanker connected by a hose; insulated vans stand nearby. The footbridge had been dismantled and passengers had to cross the track on the level. The triangle was severed from 30th January 1966, after which the Churnet platforms were left for terminating services and parcels workings until July 1968, when they too were removed. Note the fitted vans in the Up Siding delivering pharmaceutical supplies from Beeston to Boots Warehouse immediately on the left. (R.Humm coll.)

6.   A view from 22nd April 2016 records the 11.07 Crewe to Derby, but it is showing the wrong destination. A new footbridge came into use in 2013 and passengers could then reach the racecourse safely. Privatisation brought Central Trains to operate the route from 2nd March 1997. East Midlands Trains was the franchisee from 11th November 2007. (A.C.Hartless)

UTTOXETER DOVE BANK

7.   The station was on the north side of the Derby Road level crossing and was in use from 13th June 1849 until 1st October 1891. To the north of it were the 1897 short sidings to the town's 1838 gas works, which curved west from the main line. In 1913 it processed 2,755 tons of coal, rising to 4,484 in 1938 and about 7,700 tons in 1953. To the north was Spath Crossing, which was the first on BR to be automated. Its lifting barriers were operating from 5th February 1961. (J.Alsop coll.)

UTTOXETER JUNCTION.

Distance from station, 1¾ mile.
A telegraph station.
HOTELS.—White Hart; Lion.
MARKET DAY.—Wednesday.
FAIRS.—Tuesday before Old Candlemas, May 6th, July 31st, Sept. 1st and 19th, Nov. 11th and 27th.
    This is a pleasant market town, with a population of 3,645. Here is a fine church, lately rebuilt, except the old spire, which is 179 feet high; *Free Grammar School*, founded by Allen, the mathematician, in 1570, a native, and a curious six-arched stone bridge. Sir S. Degge, the antiquary, and Lord Gardner, the sailor, were natives. In the vicinity is *Hollingbury House*, the Mynor's old seat.

Extract from *Bradshaw's Guide 1866*, as seen on TV. (Reprinted by Middleton Press)

Other views and details of the extensive industrial sidings can be found in pictures 28 to 39 of the *Derby to Stoke-on-Trent* album.

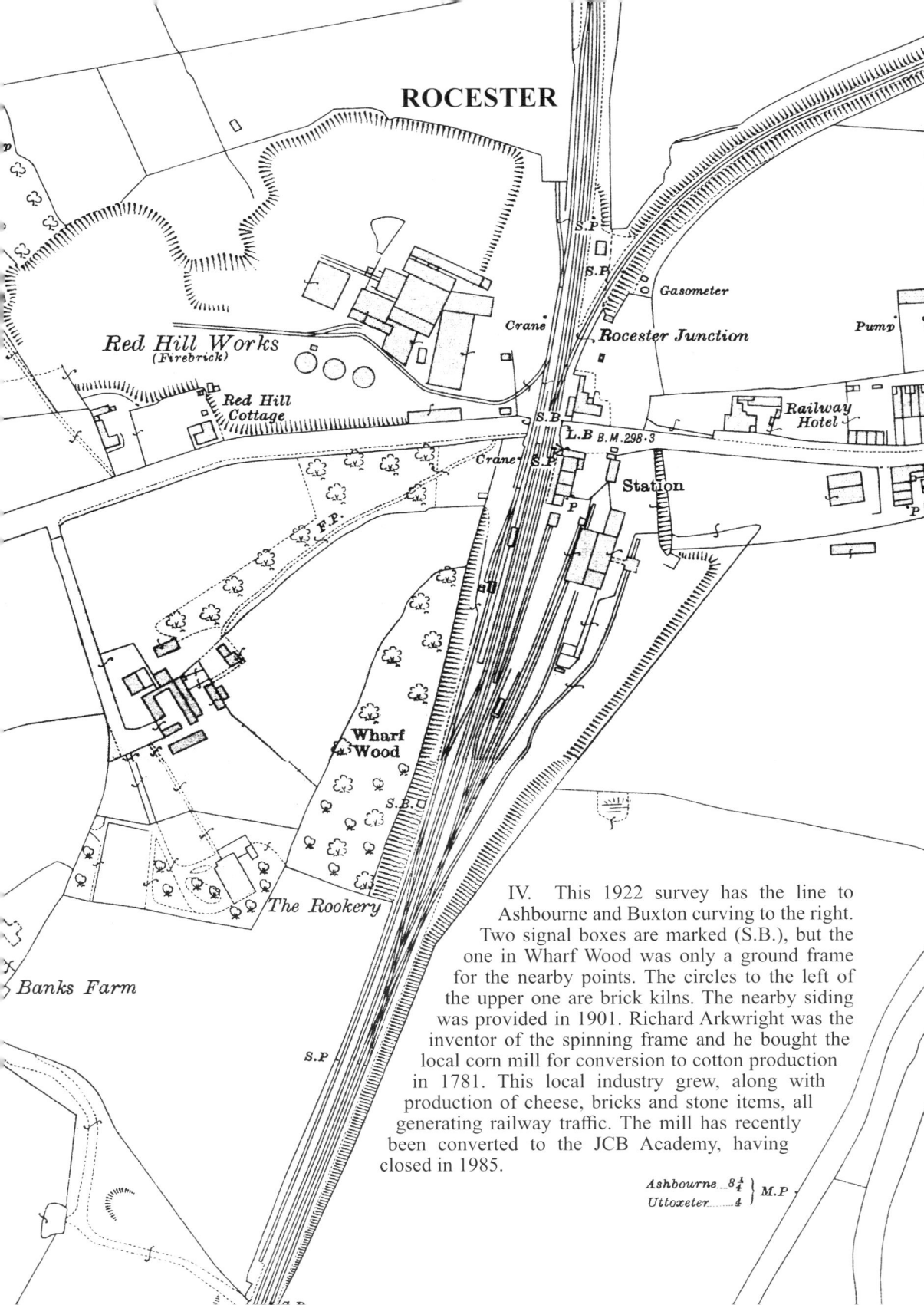

ROCESTER

Red Hill Works
(Firebrick)

Red Hill
Cottage

Crane

S.P

S.B

Gasometer

Rocester Junction

Pump

Railway
Hotel

L.B B.M.298.3

Crane S.P

Station

P

F.P.

Wharf
Wood

S.B.

The Rookery

Banks Farm

S.P

IV. This 1922 survey has the line to
Ashbourne and Buxton curving to the right.
Two signal boxes are marked (S.B.), but the
one in Wharf Wood was only a ground frame
for the nearby points. The circles to the left of
the upper one are brick kilns. The nearby siding
was provided in 1901. Richard Arkwright was the
inventor of the spinning frame and he bought the
local corn mill for conversion to cotton production
in 1781. This local industry grew, along with
production of cheese, bricks and stone items, all
generating railway traffic. The mill has recently
been converted to the JCB Academy, having
closed in 1985.

Ashbourne $8\frac{1}{4}$
Uttoxeter 4 $\Big\}$ M.P

8.   This view is eastwards and has the Railway Hotel in the background. It is not clear that there are three tracks across the road here and that there is a hand-worked crane on the right. It was rated at 5-tons capacity. A 10-ton one was north of the level crossing. They were used for loading stone mainly. The signal box had 36 levers and was in use from August 1882 until 21st May 1965. (R.Humm coll.)

9.   The awning on the right replaced the original one in 1894. It was pitched, similar to the one on the left. The train is signalled for the Leek line in this view from about 1930. On the right are end doors, used at end docks by horse boxes and milk vans. (J.Alsop coll.)

10. We witness ex-LMS class 4P 2-6-4T no. 2543 on 22nd May 1948, shortly before being renumbered. It is working the 4.22pm Leek to Uttoxeter service. On the right are the goods shed and stables. On the extreme right is the grain warehouse. Only the platform on the right was used after 1959. (W.A.Camwell/SLS)

11. Splendid provision was made for both staff and passengers. A separate house was built for the station master, behind the signal box, in 1883. Goods traffic ceased here on 1st June 1964 and ended for passengers on 4th January 1965. (J.Alsop coll.)

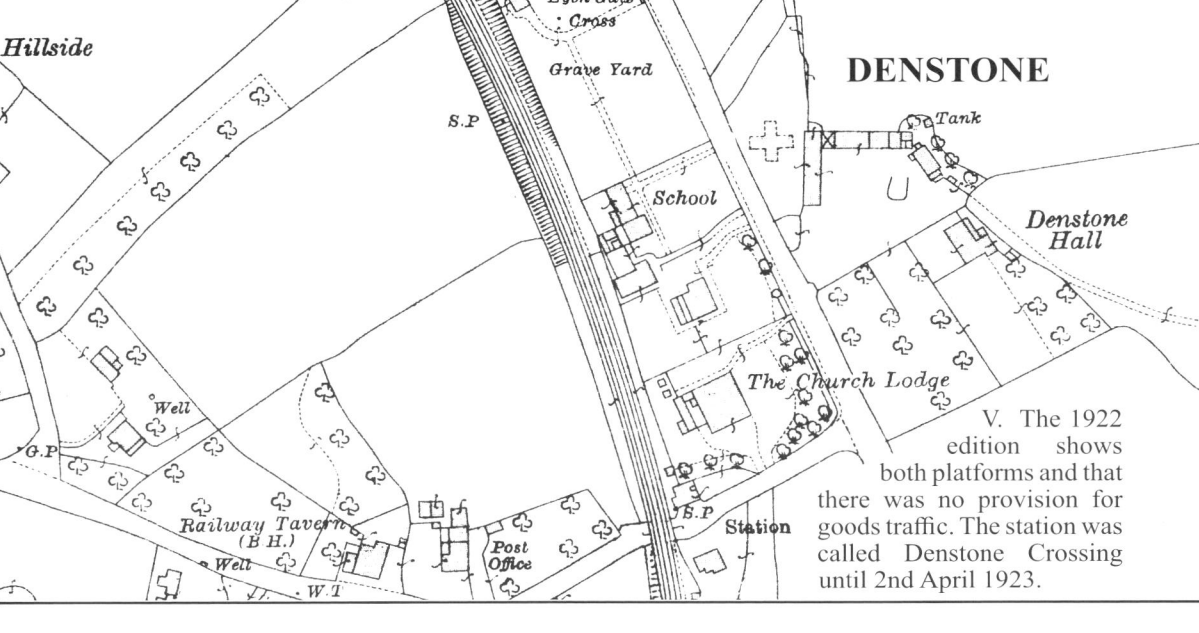

All Saints' Church
Lych Gate
Cross

Grave Yard

DENSTONE

Tank

School

Denstone
Hall

Hillside

S.P

The Church Lodge

V. The 1922 edition shows both platforms and that there was no provision for goods traffic. The station was called Denstone Crossing until 2nd April 1923.

Well

G.P

Railway Tavern
(B.H.)

Well

S.P

Station

Post
Office

W.T

12. The timber-framed crossing house was built with the line in 1849, but the station did not open until 1st August 1873, ready to serve the new Denstone College. The brick building supporting fire buckets was probably added for parcels. The rodding tunnel suggests that the six signal levers were behind the black panel. They were out of use from 21st January 1965. (R.Humm coll.)

13. Class 4P 2-6-4T no. 42381 is departing south in about 1948. Station closure came with the line on 4th January 1965. The All Saints' Church spire, of 1862, is above the middle coach. The village housed 671 in 1901, 649 in 1961 and 1220 in 2011. (W.A.Camwell/SLS)

ALTON TOWERS

VI. The 1922 edition contains much historic detail, but Alton Towers is beyond the top left border. The Lodge at its drive entrance is recorded. The goods yard was added in 1857, and enlarged in 1860 and in 1874, for the industries shown. There was also a wire mill, a paper maker and a paint manufacturer. There was still a copper works in the village in 1914. Three cranes are shown; the biggest was rated at 8 tons.

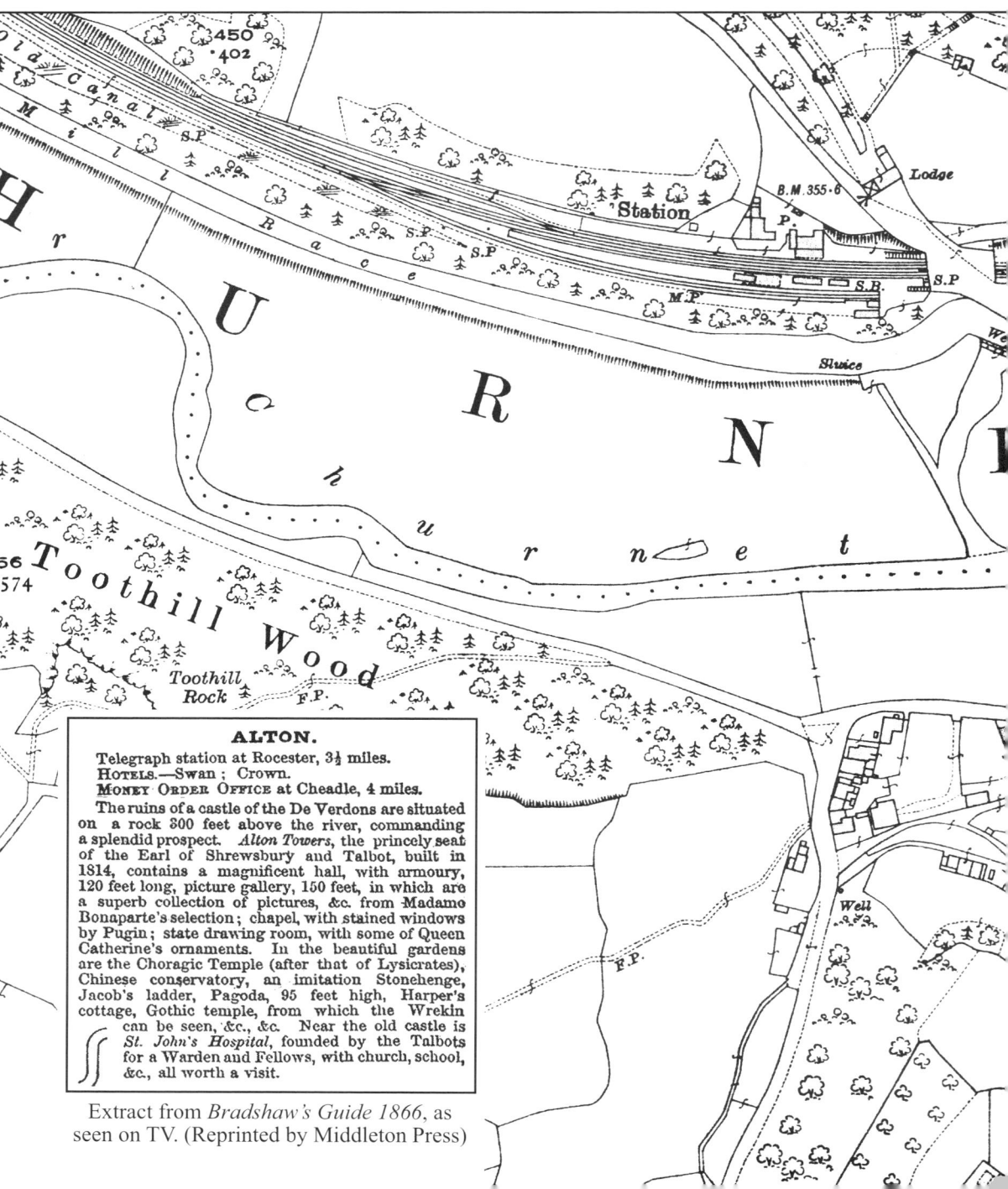

ALTON.

Telegraph station at Rocester, 3½ miles.

HOTELS.—Swan ; Crown.

MONEY ORDER OFFICE at Cheadle, 4 miles.

The ruins of a castle of the De Verdons are situated on a rock 300 feet above the river, commanding a splendid prospect. *Alton Towers*, the princely seat of the Earl of Shrewsbury and Talbot, built in 1814, contains a magnificent hall, with armoury, 120 feet long, picture gallery, 150 feet, in which are a superb collection of pictures, &c. from Madame Bonaparte's selection ; chapel, with stained windows by Pugin ; state drawing room, with some of Queen Catherine's ornaments. In the beautiful gardens are the Choragic Temple (after that of Lysicrates), Chinese conservatory, an imitation Stonehenge, Jacob's ladder, Pagoda, 95 feet high, Harper's cottage, Gothic temple, from which the Wrekin can be seen, &c., &c. Near the old castle is *St. John's Hospital*, founded by the Talbots for a Warden and Fellows, with church, school, &c., all worth a visit.

Extract from *Bradshaw's Guide 1866*, as seen on TV. (Reprinted by Middleton Press)

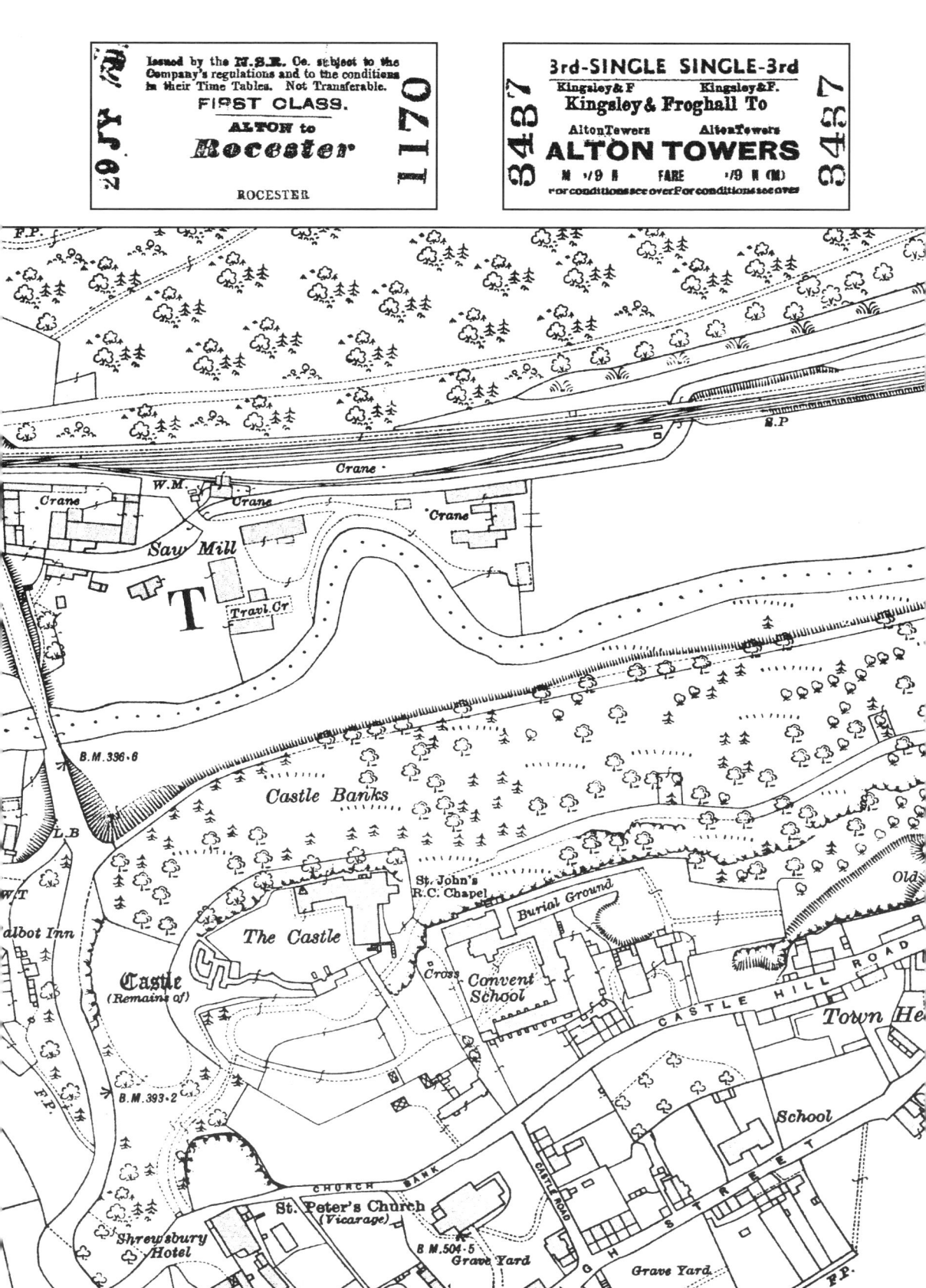

F.P.

W.M.

Crane

Crane   Crane

Crane

Saw Mill

T

Travl. Cr

B.M.336·6

Castle Banks

L.B

W.T

St. John's
R.C. Chapel

Burial Ground

Old

dlbot Inn

The Castle

Cross

Convent
School

Town He

Castle
(Remains of)

CASTLE HILL ROAD

F.P.

B.M.393·2

School

CHURCH BANK

CASTLE ROAD

STREET

St. Peter's Church
(Vicarage)

Shrewsbury
Hotel

B.M.504·5
Grave Yard

Grave Yard

F.P.

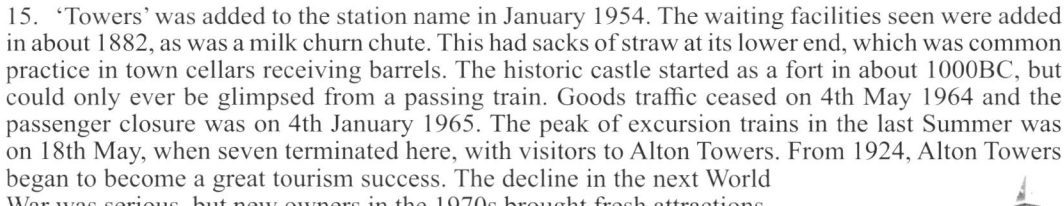

14. The station was a different style from the others on the route, at the request of the Earl of Shrewsbury. In this and the next view is the massive luggage lift close to the stairway. Its top doorway was used as a sentry post by the Home Guard during part of World War II. The lift was demanded by the Earl. (J.Alsop coll.)

15. 'Towers' was added to the station name in January 1954. The waiting facilities seen were added in about 1882, as was a milk churn chute. This had sacks of straw at its lower end, which was common practice in town cellars receiving barrels. The historic castle started as a fort in about 1000BC, but could only ever be glimpsed from a passing train. Goods traffic ceased on 4th May 1964 and the passenger closure was on 4th January 1965. The peak of excursion trains in the last Summer was on 18th May, when seven terminated here, with visitors to Alton Towers. From 1924, Alton Towers began to become a great tourism success. The decline in the next World
War was serious, but new owners in the 1970s brought fresh attractions,
inside and out, including a model railway. (J.Alsop coll.)

16.   A panorama from July 1960 includes an excursion train in the bay platform and three passengers about to use the through train signalled into the adjacent one. The bay could accommodate 10 coaches; the field to the north of the station was used for crowd control. (R.Humm coll.)

17.   The River Churnet was prone to cause difficulties here, this example being in 1961. The signal box had 30 levers and was worked until 25th January 1965. The site became the property of the Landmark Trust who undertook extensive tree clearance and building maintenance in 2009. (A.Dudman coll.)

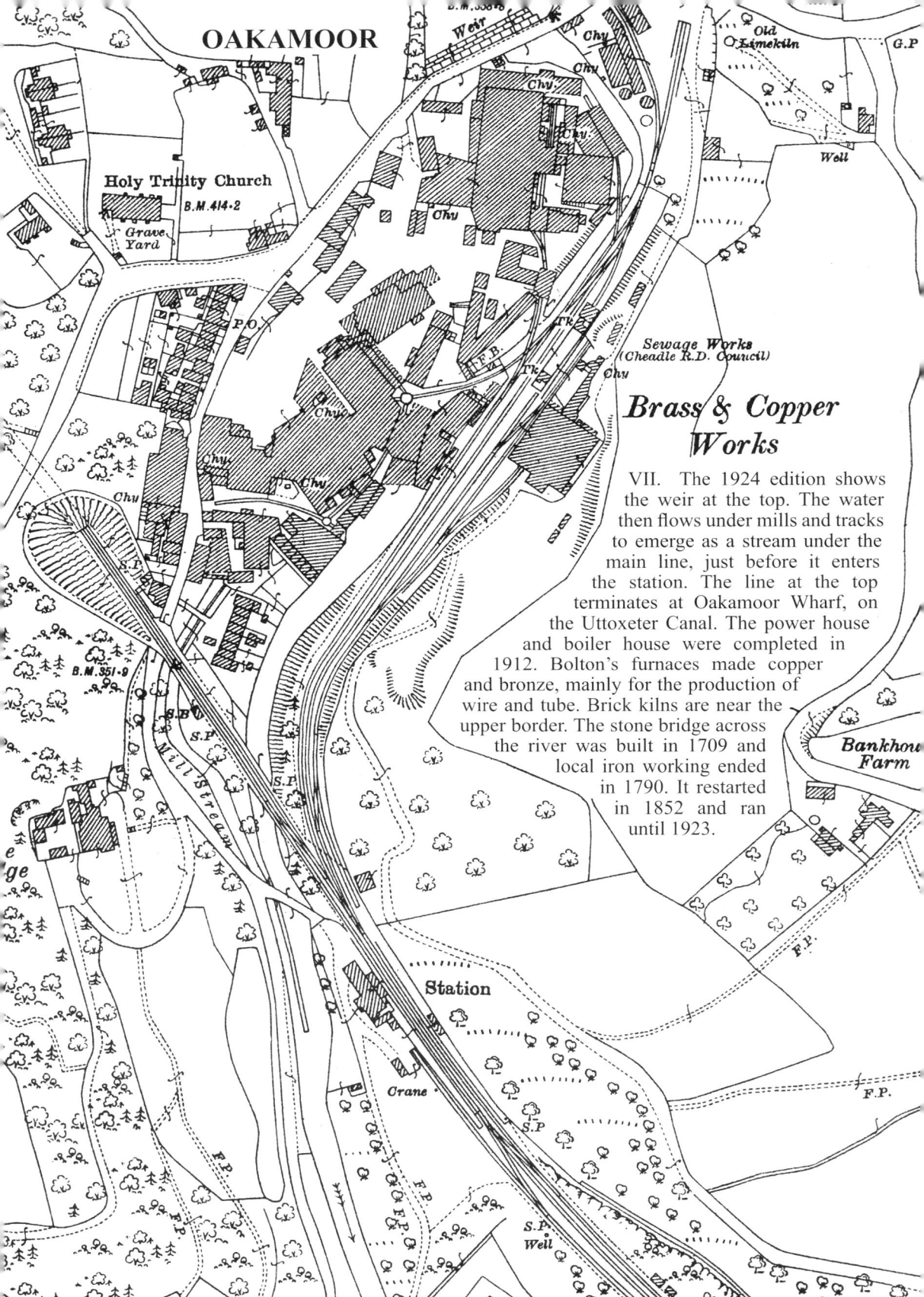

OAKAMOOR

Holy Trinity Church

B.M.414.2

Grave Yard

P.O.

Sewage Works
(Cheadle R.D. Council)

Brass & Copper Works

VII. The 1924 edition shows
the weir at the top. The water
then flows under mills and tracks
to emerge as a stream under the
main line, just before it enters
the station. The line at the top
terminates at Oakamoor Wharf, on
the Uttoxeter Canal. The power house
and boiler house were completed in
1912. Bolton's furnaces made copper
and bronze, mainly for the production of
wire and tube. Brick kilns are near the
upper border. The stone bridge across
the river was built in 1709 and
local iron working ended
in 1790. It restarted
in 1852 and ran
until 1923.

Bankhou Farm

B.M.351·9

Mill Stream

Station

Crane

18. A class B NSR 2-4-2T is departing with a mixture of four- and six-wheeled coaches before the alterations to the station in about 1900. The view is southwards. The 5-ton crane is near the station. (J.Alsop coll.)

19. No. 68 was an 0-6-0 built by the NSR at Stoke-on-Trent in 1875, devoid of a cab roof. The bi-directional signals have their lamps part way down the post. The orignal pre-1916 signal box is on the platform. (J.Alsop coll.)

20. No. 145 was a class D 0-6-0T and it has just left the tunnel, while two animals show no interest and the signal returns to danger. The curve to the factories is on the right. (R.Humm coll.)

UTTOXETER, LEEK AND MACCLESFIELD — Weekdays only.

Miles							SO		SO	WO		SO					SX	SO
		a.m.		a.m.	a.m.		a.m.		p.m.	p.m.		p.m.		p.m.		p.m.	p.m.	p.m.
0	**UTTOXETER** dep	6 20	...	6 55	8 15	...	11 45	...	...	2 50	...	3 0	...	4 40	...	...	6 0	6 10
4¼	Rocester	6 27	.	7 3	8 23	.	11 52	.	.	2 57	.	3 7	.	4 48	.	.	6 7	6 17
5¼	Denstone dep	6 30	...	7 6	8 26	...	11 55	...	...	3 0	...	3 10	...	4 51	...	...	6 10	6 20
8	Alton Towers	6 36	.	7 12	8 32	.	12 1	.	.	3 6	.	3 16	.	4 57	.	.	6 16	6 26
9¾	Oakamoor	6 42	...	7 17	8 37	...	12 5	...	...	3 10	...	3 20	...	5 4	...	...	6 21	6 31
12¼	Kingsley & Froghall	6 48	.	7 23	8 44	.	12 11	.	.	3 16	.	3 26	.	5 11	.	.	6 27	6 37
14¼	Consall	6 53	...	7 28	8 49	...	12 16	...	...	3 21	...	3 31	...	5 16	...	...	6 32	6 42
16½	Cheddleton	6 58	.	7 33	8 54	.	12 21	.	.	3 26	.	3 36	.	5 20	.	.	6 36	6 46
19	Leek arr	7 5	...	7 40	9 1	...	12 28	...	...	3 33	...	3 43	...	5 27	...	...	6 43	6 53
	Leek dep	7 8	.	7 46	9 5	.	12 32	.	1 35	3 36	.	3 46	.	.	.	6 0	6 48	6 58
21	Rudyard Lake	7 11	...	7 49	9 8	...	12 35	...	1 38	3 39	...	3 49	...	...	...	6 3	6 51	7 1
23½	Cliffe Park Halt	.	.	7 55	.	.	12 41	.	1 44	3 45	.	3 55	.	.	.	6 9	.	.
24	Rushton	7 19	...	8 0	9 15	...	12 45	...	1 47	3 48	...	3 58	...	...	...	6 12	7 0	7 10
26	Bosley	7 24	.	8 5	9 20	.	12 50	.	1 52	3 53	.	4 3	.	.	.	6 17	.	.
27¾	North Rode	7 28	...	8 9	9 24	...	12 57	...	1 57	3 57	...	4 7	...	...	...	6 21	7 8	7 18
32½	**MACCLESFIELD** (Central) arr	**7 37**	.	**8 18**	.	.	**1 6**	.	**2 7**	**4 6**	.	**4 16**	.	.	.	**6 30**	**7 17**	**7 27**
32¾	**MACCLESFIELD** (Hibel Road) ,,	**7 A49**	...	**8 20**	**9 33**	...	**1 8**	...	**2 9**	**4 8**	...	**4 18**	...	...	...	**6 32**	**7 19**	**7 29**
44¼	105 STOCKPORT (Edgeley) arr	8 26		9 10	9 55	.	1 56	.	3 15	5 6	.	5 6	.	.	.	7 30	7 52	8 15
50	105 MANCHESTER (London Road) ,,	8 38	...	9 23	10 4	...	2 13	...	3 24	5B22	...	5 15	...	...	...	7 40	8 6	8 24

A—Change at Macclesfield (Central).
B—Manchester (Mayfield).
D—Change at North Rode.
H—Arrives Macclesfield Central 6.31 a.m.

SO—Saturdays only.
SX—Saturdays excepted.
TC—Through Carriage.
WO—Wednesdays only.
WSO—Wednesdays and Saturdays only.

September 1957

21.   A southward panorama from above the tunnel mouth has the level crossing in the foreground, with the branch on the left and the station in the distance. The signal box was to be built, lower right. It had a 28-lever frame, which served from 1916 until May 1960. A ground frame lasted until closure in 1988. (J.Alsop coll.)

22.   Noted for innovation, Bolton's had a fireless 0-4-0 built for internal use, by the LNWR at their Crewe Works in 1880. It had no fire and no water tanks. It obtained steam, when required, from the boilers within the works. It appears that this model could be driven from either end. The 'boiler' simply acted as a steam store. It is numbered 3412. (A.Dudman coll.)

23. The copper wire was mainly for the electrical industry and the output grew enormously, particularly as the National Grid expanded. This demanded heavy wires in great continuous lengths. This consignment was to span the River Thames, near Dagenham in 1932. The battery electric locomotive was built by the NSR in 1917 for use at Bolton's Works, which it did until 1962. However, it also undertook local shunting of all types, having received the BR no. of B.E.L.2. It was always recharged in its shed, next to the works. The factory was demolished in 1967, having closed in 1963. (A.Dudman coll.)

24. The curved line into the works was known as the 'Wing Line' and is lower left in this view from May 1950. The running-in board on the left was an ex-LMS style known as 'Hawkseye'. (R.Humm coll.)

25.　The main building is seen again on 19th August 1963. Class 4MT 2-6-4T no. 42663 is blowing off ready to depart with the 4.13pm Uttoxeter to Leek service. (Colour-Rail.com)

26.　The same locomotive is seen on the same day, running in the opposite direction and passing the Wing connection. A Leek departure is about to enter Oakamoor Tunnel, which is 497yds in length. (Colour-Rail.com)

27. This undated view is not long before the closure to passengers on 4th January 1965. General freight ceased on 4th May 1964, but mineral traffic continued. Sadly, the splendid historic buildings did not remain for long. This photo is pre-1961 as the ground signals were altered when the Sand Siding was installed and signalling alterations carried out between Oakamoor and Froghall. (J.Alsop coll.)

28. Sidings for British Industrial Sand were in use from about May 1961 until 30th August 1988. The 'Knotty Rambler' railtour on 24th May 1972 gave an opportunity to visit the site. The sand came by the conveyor on the right, from Moneystone Quarry. Extra sidings were added in the Winter of 1960-61 for this traffic. (Colour-Rail.com)

29.   Nos 20188 and 20121 depart from the loading terminal with the 15.35 sand train to Longport on 27th August 1986. It would continue its journey the next day as the 05.03 Longport-St. Helens. The PAA air-braked hoppers had been introduced on this train a few months earlier, at the same time as the flows from Oakamoor to Wigan and Worksop ceased. This is the loading point for industrial sand for glass-making. Until 1986, trains ran to St. Helens, Wigan and Worksop, using vacuum-braked hopper wagons. The last Oakamoor-St. Helens train ran on 30th August 1988. The line was officially out of use from 6th December 1992 and closed on 17th May 1993, but it remained in place. Note the former up and down main lines in the foreground remaining in use as sidings. (P.D.Shannon)

30.   Photographed on 17th June 1988 was an 0-4-0 diesel hydraulic locomotive, which carried the name *Cammell*; seen here under the sand loader. It arrived in the Spring of 1981 from Cammell Laird Shipbuilders, Birkenhead. It was later transferred from Oakamoor to Cheddleton. The white sand covering the site gives the impression of a snow scene. Its companion was *Brightside*, which came in 1968. Both were in use here until 1988 and became CVR property in 1998. (N.Allsop)

31. It is 10th January 2010 and a sand loading re-enactment is in progress. The driver of no. 25322 *Tamworth Castle* is watching carefully, although gravel wagons are in use. Most of the sand was destined for Pilkington's Glass Works at St. Helens. (D.Gibson)

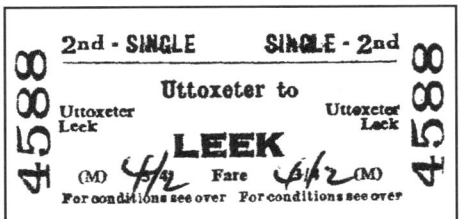

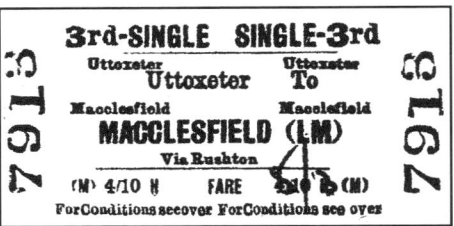

LEEK AND UTTOXETER
WEEKDAYS ONLY

Miles			SO	SX			Miles				SO	SX
		a.m.	a.m.	p.m.						a.m.	a.m.	p.m.
0	LEEK .... dep	6 30	11 25	4 28	.		0	UTTOXETER .... dep	6 20	7 55	11 18	4 13
2¼	Cheddleton	6 34	11 29	4 32	.		4½	Rocester	6 27	8 2	11 25	4 21
3½	Consall	6 38	11 33	4 36	.		5½	Denstone	6 30	8 5	11 28	4 24
5¼	Kingsley and Froghall	6 53	11 39	4 44	...		8	Alton Towers	6 36	8 11	11 34	4 30
8½	Oakamoor	6 58	11 46	4 49	.		9½	Oakamoor	6 42	8 15	11 38	4 37
11	Alton Towers	7 2	11 50	4 53	.		12½	Kingsley and Froghall	6 54	8 20	11 44	4 44
13¾	Denstone	7 7	11 55	4 58	.		14½	Consall	6 59	8 25	11 49	4 49
14¾	Rocester	7 10	11 58	5 1	...		16¾	Cheddleton	7 4	8 30	11 54	4 53
19	UTTOXETER .... arr	7 19	12 7	5 10	.		19	LEEK .... arr	7 11	8 37	12 1	5 0

SO—Saturdays only.

SX—Saturdays excepted.

September 1964

KINGSLEY & FROGHALL

VIII. This 1924 extract is a little to the west of the station and continues on the next map, where the latter is shown.

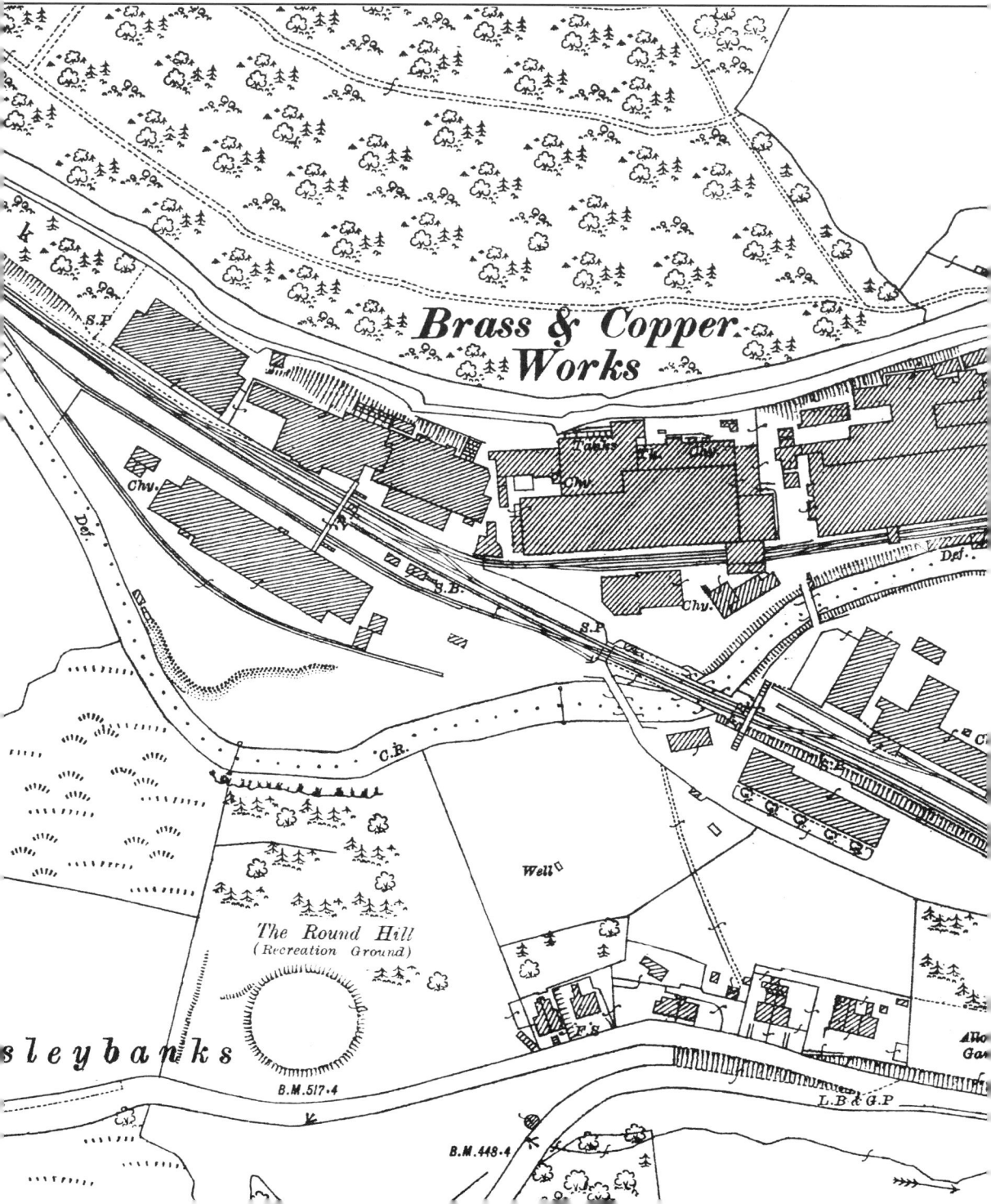

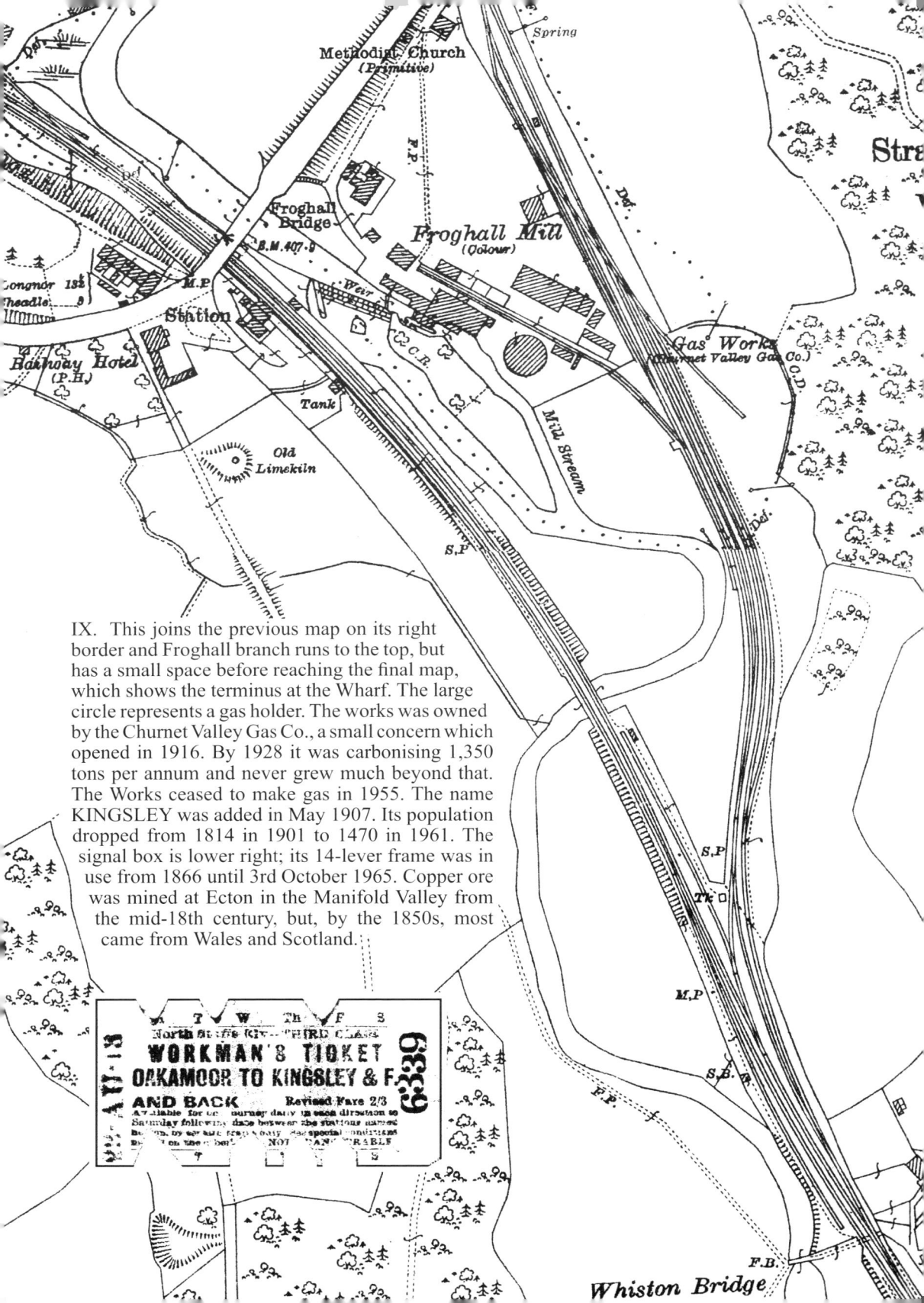

Spring

Methodist Church
(Primitive)

Froghall
Bridge

Froghall Mill
(Colour)

B.M. 407·9

Congnor 15¾
Theadle

M.P.

Weir

Station

Gas Works
(Churnet Valley Gas Co.)

Railway Hotel
(P.H.)

Tank

C.B.

Old
Limekiln

Mill Stream

S.P.

IX. This joins the previous map on its right
border and Froghall branch runs to the top, but
has a small space before reaching the final map,
which shows the terminus at the Wharf. The large
circle represents a gas holder. The works was owned
by the Churnet Valley Gas Co., a small concern which
opened in 1916. By 1928 it was carbonising 1,350
tons per annum and never grew much beyond that.
The Works ceased to make gas in 1955. The name
KINGSLEY was added in May 1907. Its population
dropped from 1814 in 1901 to 1470 in 1961. The
signal box is lower right; its 14-lever frame was in
use from 1866 until 3rd October 1965. Copper ore
was mined at Ecton in the Manifold Valley from
the mid-18th century, but, by the 1850s, most
came from Wales and Scotland.

S.P.

Tk

M.P.

S.B.

F.P.

F.B.

Whiston Bridge

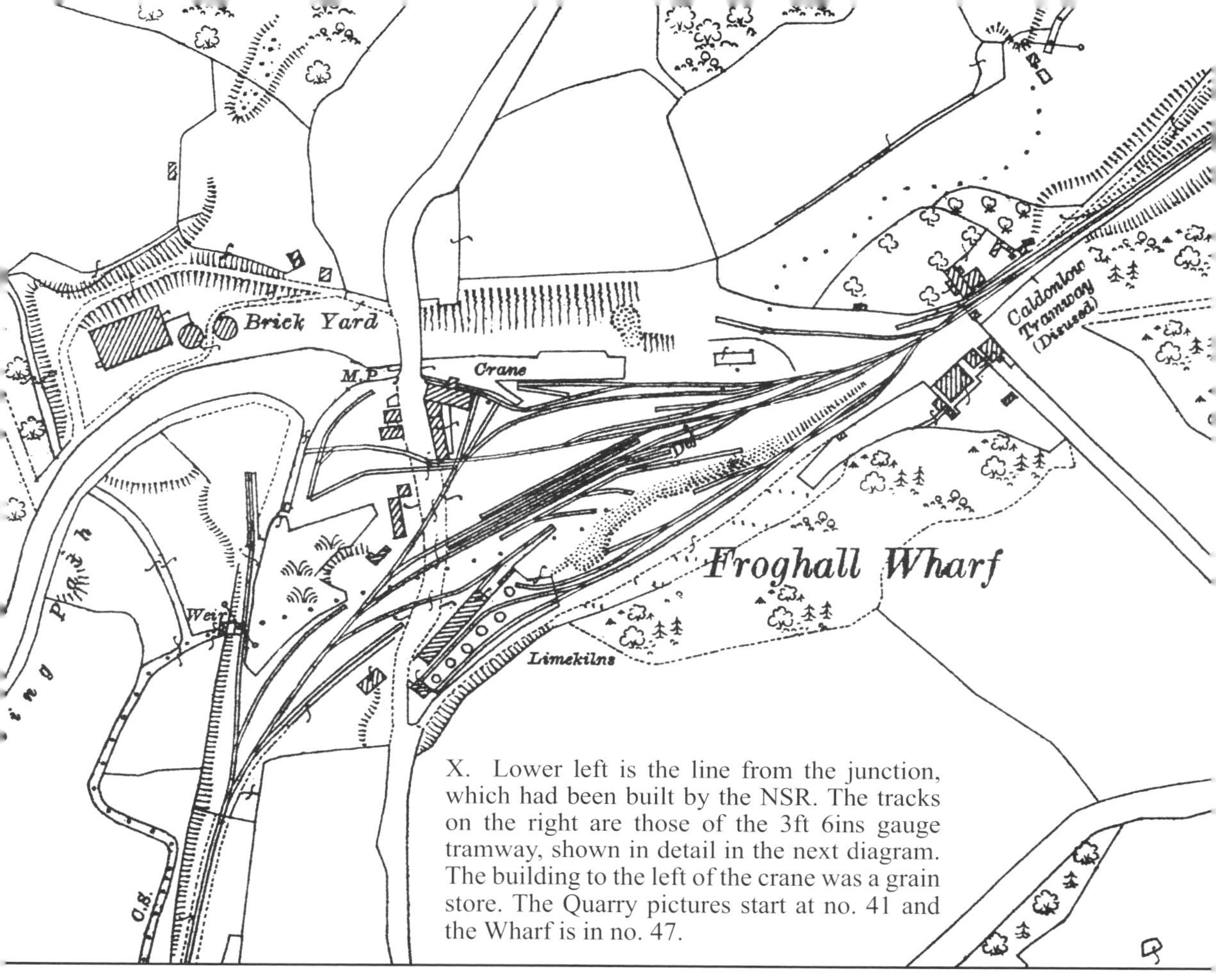

X. Lower left is the line from the junction, which had been built by the NSR. The tracks on the right are those of the 3ft 6ins gauge tramway, shown in detail in the next diagram. The building to the left of the crane was a grain store. The Quarry pictures start at no. 41 and the Wharf is in no. 47.

32. A train bound for Uttoxeter is loading passengers in about 1950. The NSR style water filler was still in use and the generous size tanks are also included. Fire buckets include the water provisions for the station. The canopy change revealed in picture 9 did not occur here. (W.A.Camwell/SLS)

33.   A 1952 panorama includes the spacious three storeys for the station master and his family, plus part of the extensive premises of Bolton's Works. This factory had a staff of over 600 by 1914 and produced mainly copper wire. The earliest buildings, in the distance, date from 1890.
(R.Humm coll.)

34.   Here we have the 11.50am (SO) Leek to Uttoxeter on 28th May 1960, hauled by class 4MT 2-6-4T no. 42454. It is one of the two-cylindered models. The valley depth has become clear. Bolton's Sidings signal box was in use from March 1918 to October 1968. It housed 38 levers.
(R.Humm coll.)

35. Sadly, the original buildings were demolished. The enterprising revivalists undertook a complete rebuild, albeit in brick rather than stone. This was the state of progress in August 2004. The view is from the bridge seen in picture 33. (D.Gibson)

36. The finished product was photographed on 8th June 2008 as no. 37075 arrived, ready to depart at 13.59. The event that day was the Alf Tunstall Classic Bus Rally. (D.Gibson)

37.   We move on to 19th August 2010 and we see the 15.29 departure for Cheddleton. It is headed by ex-LMS class 8F 2-8-0 no. 8624. Construction of this class began in 1935 and 447 were in use by June 1944. (D.Gibson)

38.   Photographers abound as usual on 1st April 2012. The variety of rolling stock constantly attracts the crowds. No. 33021 arrives at 11.53 and is seen from the platform little used by passengers. (D.Gibson)

39. Two photographs from 22nd September 2012 reveal aspects of the revival achievements. Cats Whiskers had been restored on DMUs. Here, we witness the 10.30 departure to Cheddleton. (A.Nicholls)

40. No. D8059 is starting on a rare trip to Caldon Low sidings at 15.30. It will run via Leek Brook and Ipstones, but passengers were not able to alight at stations beyond Cheddleton. Soon after departure, however, they could still see the old copper works. It was still in use in 2017, albeit with scrap metal for recycling. The Bolton's business had been expanded to here in 1890 and sidings were laid to it. (A.Nicholls)

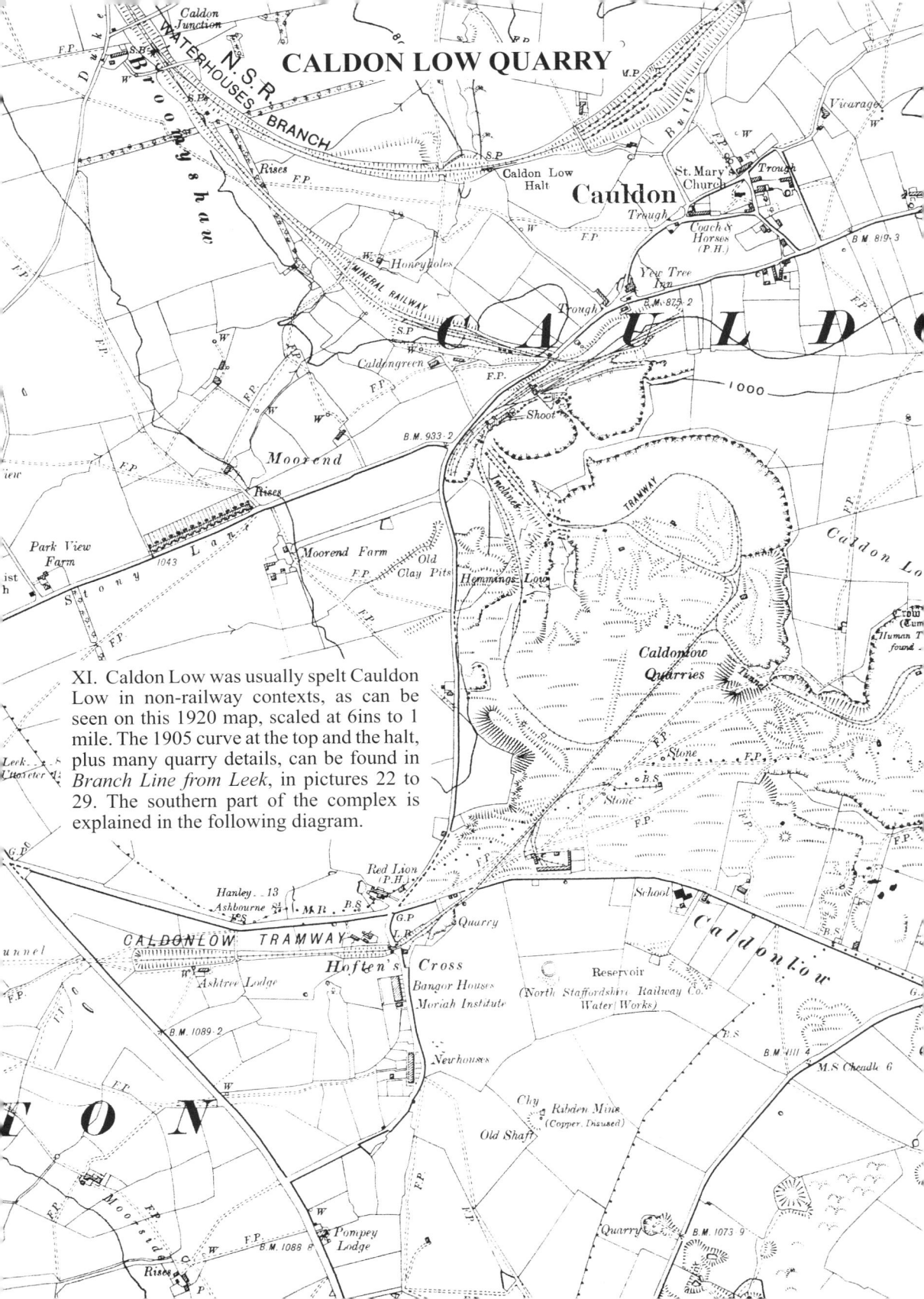

CALDON LOW QUARRY

XI. Caldon Low was usually spelt Cauldon Low in non-railway contexts, as can be seen on this 1920 map, scaled at 6ins to 1 mile. The 1905 curve at the top and the halt, plus many quarry details, can be found in *Branch Line from Leek*, in pictures 22 to 29. The southern part of the complex is explained in the following diagram.

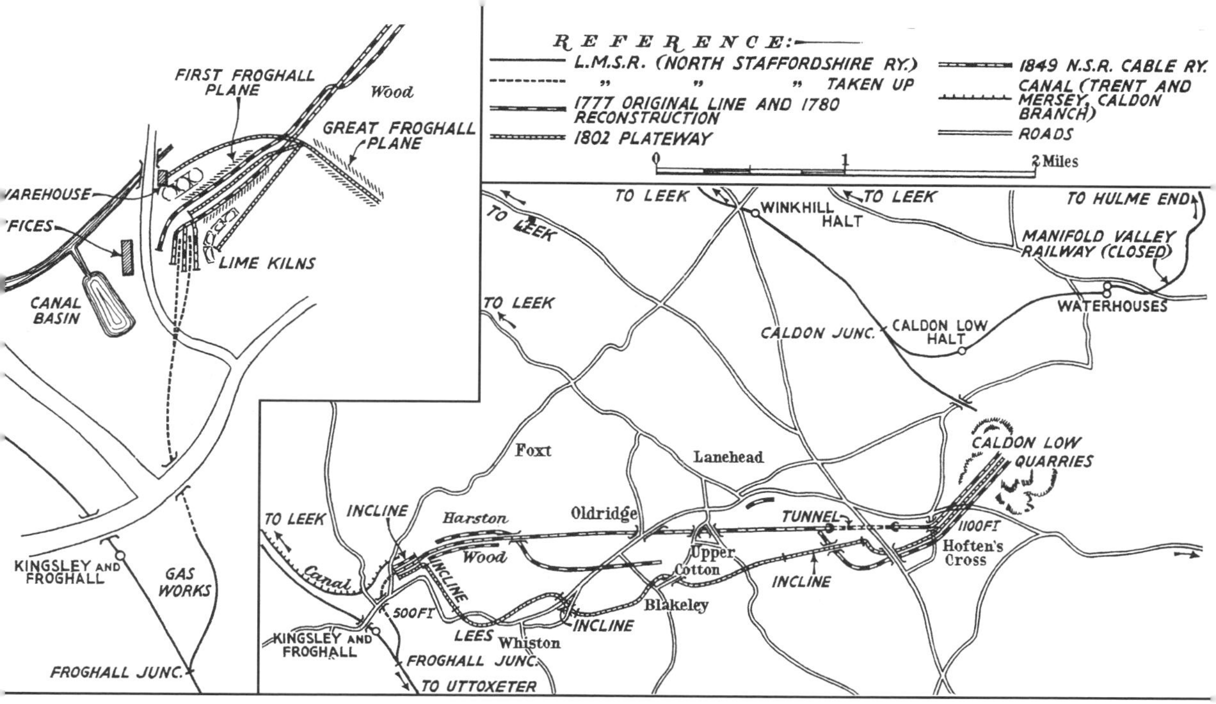

REFERENCE:—

L.M.S.R. (NORTH STAFFORDSHIRE RY.)
  "   "   "   TAKEN UP
1777 ORIGINAL LINE AND 1780 RECONSTRUCTION
1802 PLATEWAY
1849 N.S.R. CABLE RY.
CANAL (TRENT AND MERSEY, CALDON BRANCH)
ROADS

2 Miles

FIRST FROGHALL PLANE
Wood
GREAT FROGHALL PLANE
WAREHOUSE
OFFICES
LIME KILNS
CANAL BASIN

TO LEEK
TO LEEK
WINKHILL HALT
TO LEEK
TO HULME END
MANIFOLD VALLEY RAILWAY (CLOSED)
WATERHOUSES
TO LEEK
CALDON JUNC.
CALDON LOW HALT
CALDON LOW QUARRIES
Foxt
Lanehead
TO LEEK
INCLINE
Harston
Oldridge
TUNNEL
1100 FT
Wood
Upper Cotton
Hoften's Cross
Canal
INCLINE
INCLINE
Blakeley
500 FT
INCLINE
LEES
Whiston
KINGSLEY AND FROGHALL
GAS WORKS
KINGSLEY AND FROGHALL
FROGHALL JUNC.
FROGHALL JUNC.
TO UTTOXETER

XII. This diagram was published in 1937 and photographs 41 to 46 were taken in the early 1930s to show the remains. The western terminus is enlarged on the left and can be seen in more detail on map X, near picture 32 herein. The line through Oldridge closed in March 1920.
(*The Railway Magazine*)

41.   The high level tracks within the quarries are in the centre of map XI and were 3ft 6ins gauge. The two 0-4-0STs built by Henry Hughes in 1877 are seen. Nearest is *Frog,* and *Toad* is behind.
(J.Alsop coll.)

42.   A closer view of *Toad* has wet weather evident. Strong winds were also common here; the ground is over 1000ft above sea level. The third 0-4-0ST also had no cab. It was built by Bagnalls in 1901 and named *Bobs*. (J.Alsop coll.)

43.   We are on the 1849 route and close to the engine shed. The long drop sides facilitated the manual unloading of stone with shovels. Business diminished in the early 1930s. The quarry had been in the hands of the NSR from 1847 and the LMS from 1923 to 1934. It was outside the railway world thereafter. (J.Alsop coll.)

44. Hofton's Cross is shown on both the map and the diagram. The bridge is from 1849 and the track bed on the right is dated 1777 to 1802. Much of the output was crushed for road surfacing, eventually being coated with tar or bitumen. (J.Alsop coll.)

45. The tunnel contained 3ft 6ins track from its opening in 1849. Caves were discovered during quarry blasting on 24th February 1906, as a new quarry face was being prepared. Delicate tubular stalactites, 6ft in length, and a perfectly formed stalagmite, 2ft in length, were revealed in one cave. The NSR erected a staircase and promoted the spectacle as a tourist attraction. The cave was opened to the public for about two years, but was subsequently destroyed by continued quarry work by April 1908. The tunnel collapsed in 1963. (J.Alsop coll.)

46.   The diagram refers to a PLANE, which was an incline worked by a long chain running round a large horizontal drum at the top. Steel ropes were used later. Gravity supplied the power, as the loaded wagons pulled up the empty ones. This is the top of Froghall's first Plane. (J.Alsop coll.)

47.   We are now down at Froghall Canal Basin, in about 1905. This is where all the stone was loaded into barges, prior to the arrival of the railway. The details are on map X. The wharf is seen on the right and rail traffic to it ceased in the mid-1930s. Quarry output northwards and southwards continued by rail into the 1980s, but road transport has been used thereafter. Much has been used in cement production and as lime. (A.Dudman coll.)

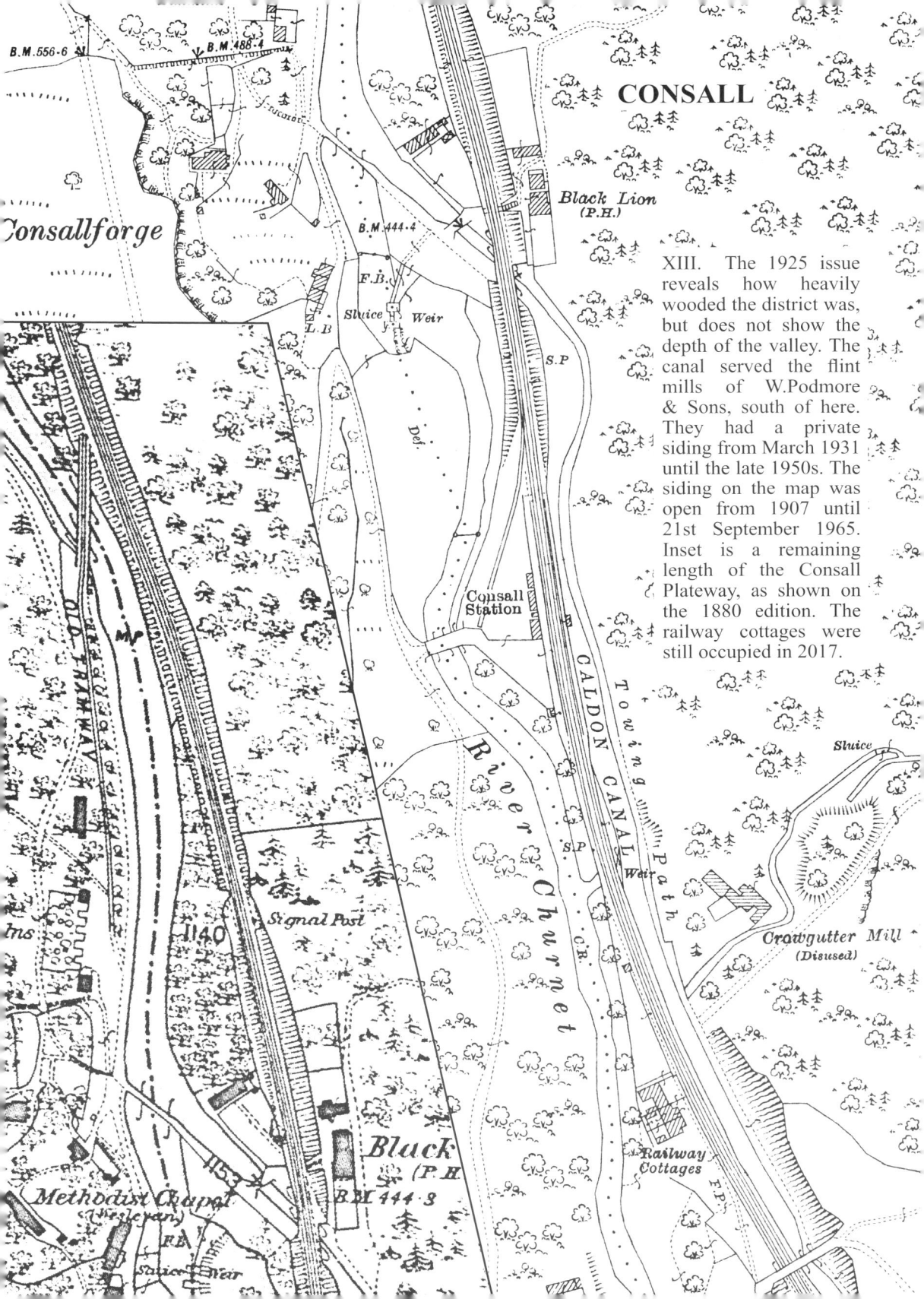

CONSALL

Black Lion (P.H.)

XIII. The 1925 issue reveals how heavily wooded the district was, but does not show the depth of the valley. The canal served the flint mills of W. Podmore & Sons, south of here. They had a private siding from March 1931 until the late 1950s. The siding on the map was open from 1907 until 21st September 1965. Inset is a remaining length of the Consall Plateway, as shown on the 1880 edition. The railway cottages were still occupied in 2017.

Consallforge

B.M.556·6

B.M.488·4

B.M.444·4

F.B.

Sluice   Weir

L.B.

S.P.

Def.

Consall Station

CALDON CANAL

Towing Path

River Churnet

S.P.

Weir

C.R.

Sluice

Crowgutter Mill
(Disused)

OLD TRAMWAY

Signal Post

1140

Railway Cottages

F.P.

Methodist Chapel
(Wesleyan)

F.A.

Black (P.H.)

B.M.444·3

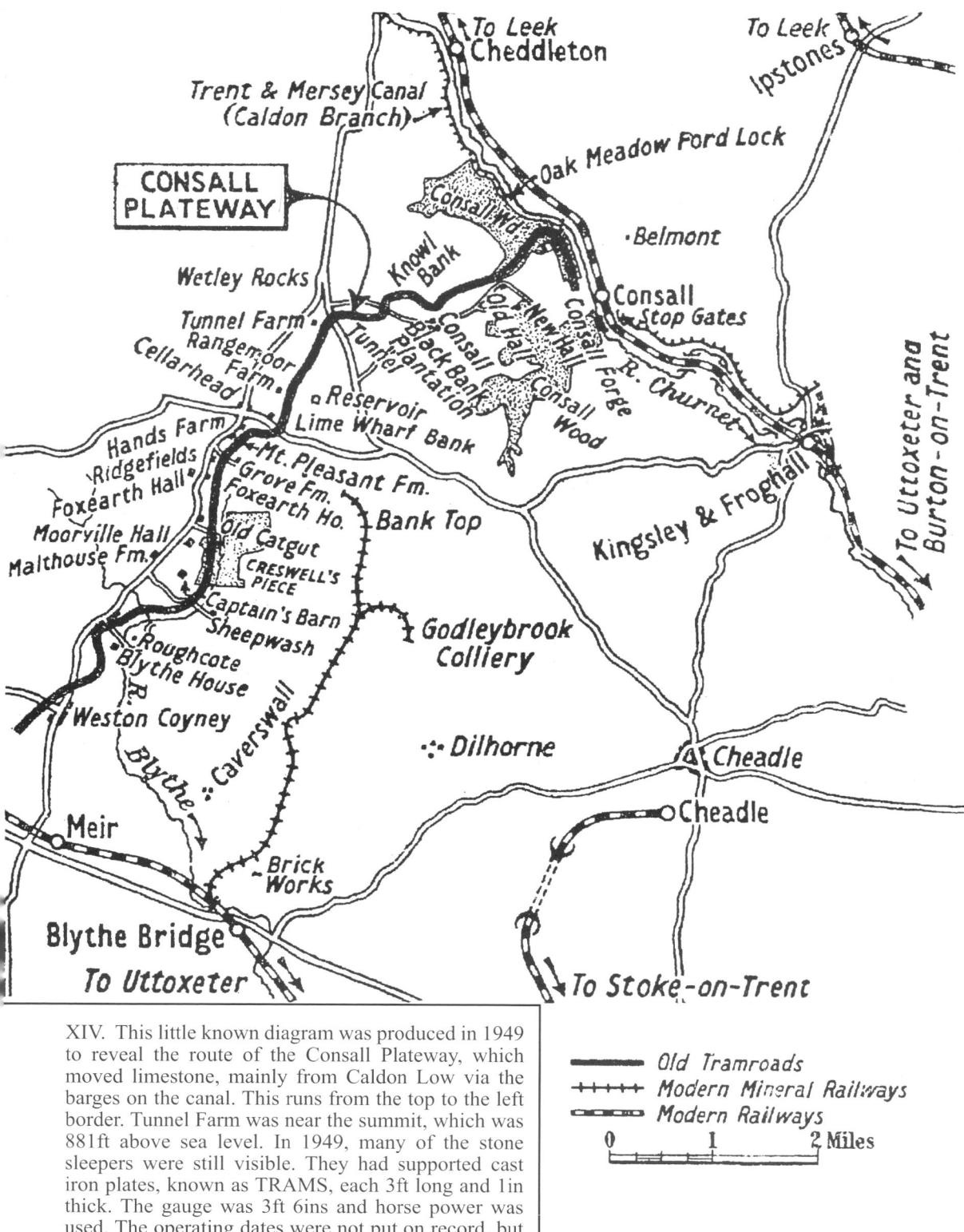

XIV. This little known diagram was produced in 1949 to reveal the route of the Consall Plateway, which moved limestone, mainly from Caldon Low via the barges on the canal. This runs from the top to the left border. Tunnel Farm was near the summit, which was 881ft above sea level. In 1949, many of the stone sleepers were still visible. They had supported cast iron plates, known as TRAMS, each 3ft long and 1in thick. The gauge was 3ft 6ins and horse power was used. The operating dates were not put on record, but closure was probably in 1848.

Map labels:

To Leek
Cheddleton
To Leek
Ipstones
Trent & Mersey Canal (Caldon Branch)
Oak Meadow Ford Lock
CONSALL PLATEWAY
Consall Wd
Belmont
Consall
Stop Gates
Wetley Rocks
Knowl Bank
New Hall
Old Hall
Consall Forge
R. Churnet
Tunnel Farm
Rangemoor Farm
Tunnel
Black Bank
Consall Plantation
Consall Wood
To Uttoxeter and Burton-on-Trent
Cellarhead
Reservoir
Lime Wharf Bank
Hands Farm
Mt. Pleasant Fm.
Ridgefields
Grove Fm.
Foxearth Hall
Foxearth Ho.
Bank Top
Kingsley & Froghall
Moorville Hall
Old Catgut
CRESWELL'S PIECE
Malthouse Fm.
Captain's Barn
Sheepwash
Godleybrook Colliery
Roughcote
Blythe House
R. Blythe
Weston Coyney
Caverswall
Dilhorne
Cheadle
Cheadle
Meir
Brick Works
Blythe Bridge
To Uttoxeter
To Stoke-on-Trent

Legend:

——— Old Tramroads
+++++ Modern Mineral Railways
▪▬▪▬ Modern Railways

0   1   2 Miles

48. This splendid panorama, from about 1910, includes a barge on the river and a 4-4-0 on a lengthy train. It is southbound, probably near the top of the map. Ironstone tips disfigure the hillside in several locations in this area; some are top right. (J.Alsop coll.)

49. NSR 2-4-0T no. 41 rattles across one of the longest lattice girder bridges on the route, with a four-wheeled coach in tow. Railings were not required until some accidents had taken place. (R.Humm coll.)

50. The boundary of the station yard is a little different from that shown on the map and the siding is not evident. The station opened on 3rd March 1902, when the population of the village was just 200. The road surface appears to be very rough. (J.Alsop coll.)

51. Class 4P 2-6-4T no. 42304 waits at the crossing used by passengers in about 1954. Passenger traffic ceased on 4th January 1965. (W.A.Camwell/SLS)

52.   Reopening took place on 11th July 1998. This splendid record is from 17th December 2005 at 11.56 and features a 'Santa & Steam' special departing north behind 2-8-0 no. 5197. It was built in 1945 for the United States Army Transportation Corp, in Ohio. With the war ending, it was sold to the Chinese State Railways and it hauled mostly coal until the mid-1990s. It has been privately owned since being imported in 1995. (D.Gibson)

53.   Although taken on 24th February 2008, this scene could easily pass for the 1960s. Class 4MT 2-6-4T no. 80098 and former Somerset & Dorset allocated class 4F 0-6-0 no. 44422 prepare to head to Froghall with a demonstration freight train. (N.Allsop)

54.   A closer view on 21st July 2013 includes the canal wall under the platform and a coach for volunteer accommodation standing on the siding, which was disconnected from the running line. No. 33102 would take the train on to Froghall at 15.20. (D.Gibson)

55.   A fine view from 17th January 2016 includes the run-round loop, which was laid in 1998. We look south and glimpse a fragment of the canal on the left. The suffix FORGE was added initially. Both buildings were replicas of the originals, but the signal box came from Clifton, near Ashbourne, via Cheddleton; see picture 60. (Colour-Rail.com)

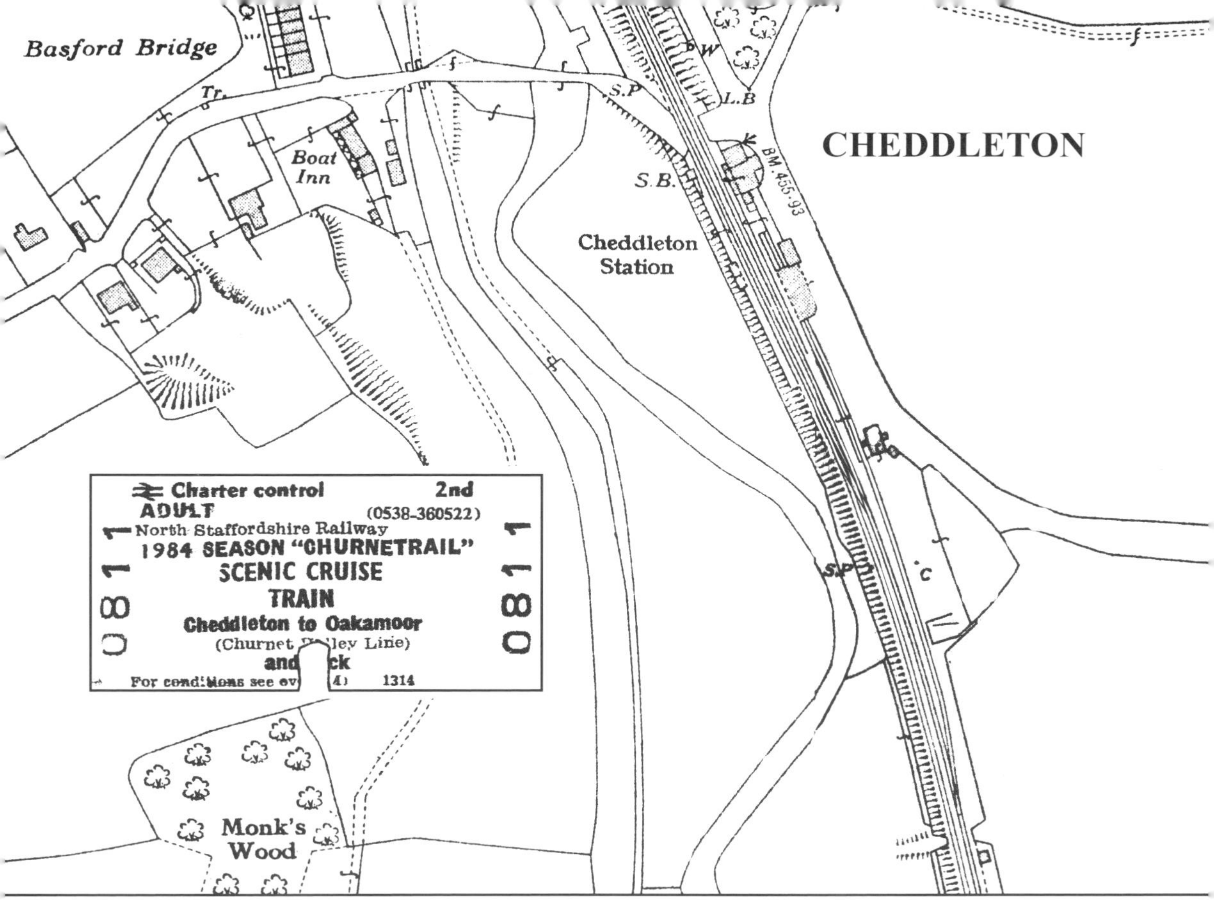

Basford Bridge

Boat Inn

CHEDDLETON

Cheddleton Station

Monk's Wood

XV. The 1937 edition has the level crossing near the top, but the 522yd long Cheddleton Tunnel was further north. It was the longest to be built on the Churnet Valley route. C marks the position of a 5-ton crane. Bridges over the river and the canal are near the top of the map. The canal declined after nationalisation in 1948, but was reopened in 1974.

56. Opening with the line, the station was graced with the usual fine architectural details. The locality housed 2562 in 1901, this rising to 5215 by 1961. It was 6311 in 2011. (J.Alsop coll.)

57. The single signal is situated away from the track to which it refers, due to visibility limitations. The shelter on the right protected traffic to and from the nearby Brittains paper mill. It, and the adjacent shed, were built in 1902. The mill was north of the station and started production in 1804, its coal coming by barge. (J.Alsop coll.)

58. Class 4MT 2-6-4T no. 42609 is being examined by the signalman dutifully on 19th December 1964. Closure to passengers took place on 4th January 1965 and on 5th April 1965 for general goods. Demolition started in May 1974, but a local councillor stopped it and 'Listing' soon followed. (Colour-Rail.com)

59. Now the signalman is being examined from the rear end, from the rear coach of a train departing south. The 1888 signal box had 19 levers and was in use until 13th October 1968. The planning permission for a railway museum here was given in November 1976. (Colour-Rail.com)

60. The reopening special ran to Oakamoor on 25th February 1984. Nos 20121 and 20188 pass the preserved station at Cheddleton with the 10.05 St. Helens-Oakamoor sand empties on 27th August 1986. After the second track had been removed in 1968, a STOP board was erected behind the camera, at the end of the platform, plus another beyond the crossing. The signal box on the left had been moved from Clifton in December 1983 and was awaiting restoration. See picture 66 for a bigger one. (P.D.Shannon)

61. No. 47322 is bound for Oakamoor with empty stock on 19th July 1988. The new engine shed and sidings had recently been built on a small area of land purchased from the local farmer. The collection gradually grew and there were 19 steaming days here in 1981. (N.Allsop)

62. Outside the shed on 22nd September 1991 is ex-LMS class 0-6-0 no. 4422 working a shuttle service to Consall with no. D7672. Standing on the right is no. D3420. The cross on the signal arm indicates that it is inactive. (A.Nicholls)

63. No. D7672 is seen in the dock siding on the same day. This was the starting point for trains to Oakamoor in the early revival days. An excursion was run from here to Llandudno on 5th June 1982 and more followed elsewhere. The first passengers were conveyed by the restorers to Oakamoor on 25th February 1984. From 1978, the group was known as the North Staffordshire Railway Society. The CVR was formed in 1992 and BR closed the route in 1993. The sale took place in March 1995 and a Light Railway Order followed on 4th May 1996, one of the last. (A.Nicholls)

64. We move to the next century and find history being repeated in fine style on 6th April 2007. Mk.I coaches are running over the level crossing at 4.0pm, hauled by BR standard class 2-6-4T no. 80098. (D.Gibson)

65.   Reference to diagram XVIII (lower) will confirm that the line occupied by the DMU on 11th July 2010 was just a terminal line after having been relaid. Departing is LMS class 8F 2-8-0 no. 8624. The gates were manually operated. (D.Gibson)

66.   The signal box came from Elton Crossing, near Sandbach, in 1976, to start the revival here. A Diesel Gala Weekend was held in September 2012 and, seen on the 22nd, is 0-6-0DE *Roger H. Bennett* (YE 2748/1959), which was ex-NCB Littleton Colliery. It was in use on the gala weekend as part of a 'Driver for a Fiver' attraction. (A.Nicholls)

67.   Seen on the same day are diesel units, nos 50455, 59701 and 50517, working the 14.07 train to Kingsley & Froghall. The bay platform appears in both photographs. (A.Nicholls)

68.   Bearing the headboard SANTA'S EXPRESS, USATC 2-8-0 no. 6046 speeds through at 13.40 on 5th November 2012. Two such engines headed the 12.20 from Froghall to Ipstones on 25th February 2017 and, on it, your author launched his *Branch Line from Leek* album. Their music was marvellous. (D.Gibson)

69. *Bellerophon* was a slayer of monsters in Greek mythology and the name given to an 0-6-0WT built in 1874 for (and by) the Haydock Collieries. It was subject to coal nationalisation in 1947 and sent for scrapping in 1964, but it was saved. It is seen on 30th June 2015, on holiday from the Foxfield Railway, which is featured in the Middleton Press *Derby to Stoke-on-Trent* album. The event is the 'Anything Goes Gala'. (D.Gibson)

70. The train is seen later the same day, with stock owned by the Vintage Carriages Trust, who had purchased *Bellerophon* for £1 in 1981. The train standing in this classical environment is the 'Knotty Charter'. The locomotive had 10 to 15 days running on the line in each of the next two years. The NSR used the Knotty symbol and one is shown on the coach. (D.Gibson)

LEEK BROOK JUNCTION

XVI. The 1937 maps are continuous, the lower part of this triangle joining the top of the next map. The route at the top of this one continues to Leek and has Leek Brook Junction North Box nearby. The line to Waterhouses is on the right. Details of this and the engine shed are in the *Branch Line from Leek* album (Middleton Press).

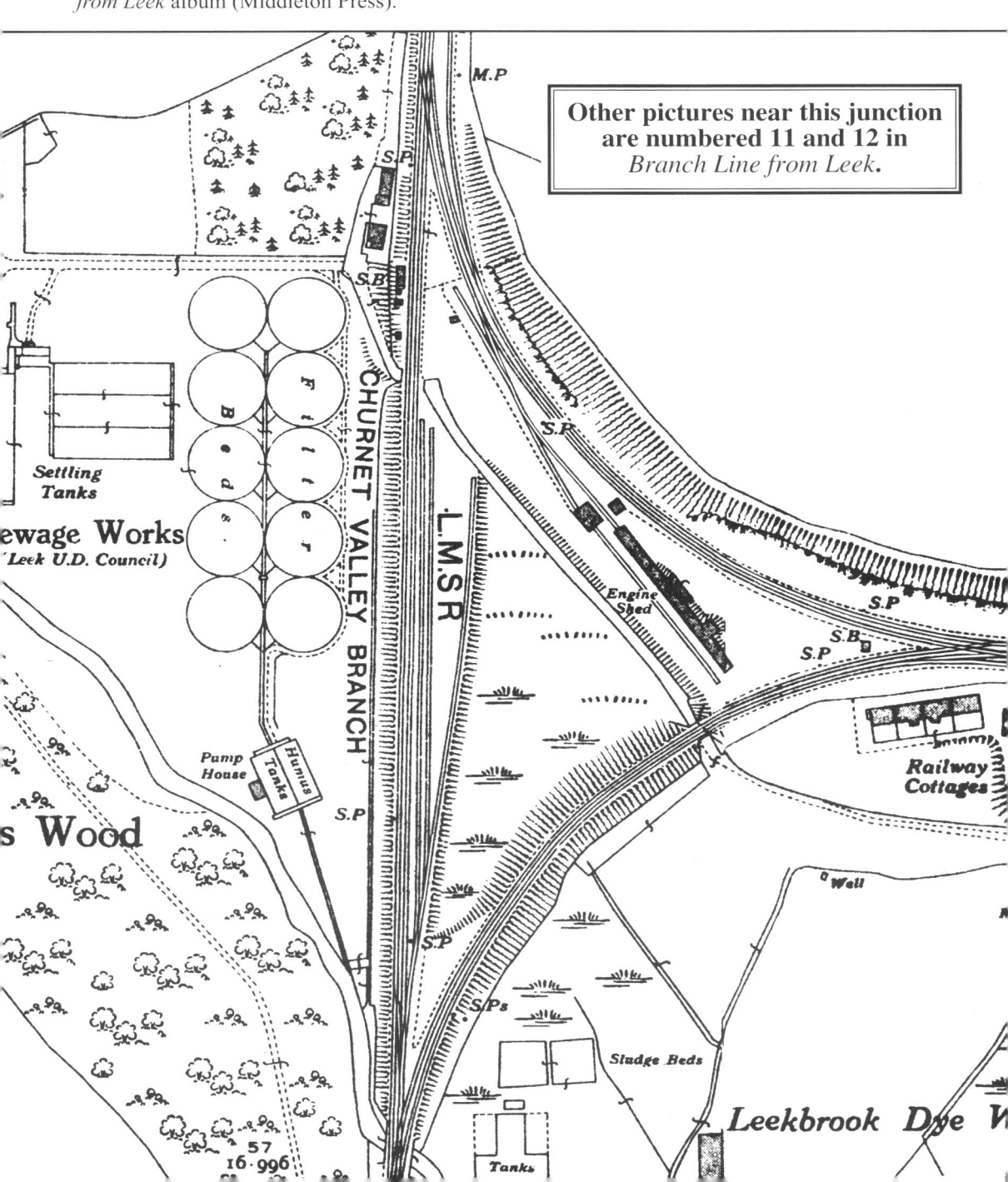

M.P

Other pictures near this junction
are numbered 11 and 12 in
Branch Line from Leek.

S.P

S.B

S.P

S.P

Settling
Tanks

F
i
l
t
e
r

B
e
d
s

CHURNET VALLEY BRANCH

L.M.S.R

Engine
Shed

S.B

S.P

ewage Works
(Leek U.D. Council)

Pump
House

Humus
Tanks

S.P

Railway
Cottages

s Wood

Well

S.P

S/Ps

Sludge Beds

Leekbrook Dye W

57
16·996

Tanks

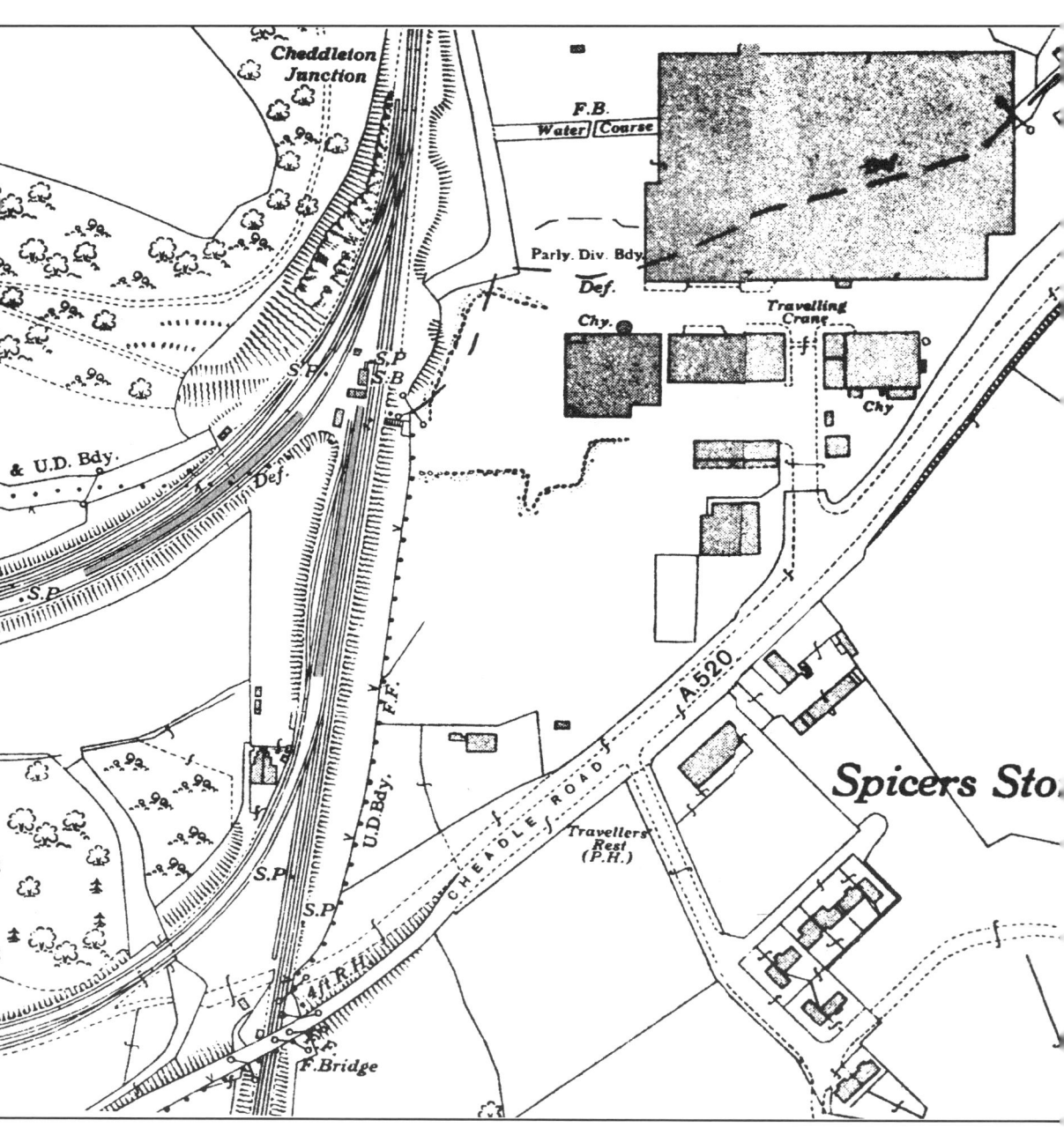

XVII. The upper curve on the left is destined for Stoke-on-Trent and has a platform between the two running lines. There is a straight one to the right of it. Both served St. Edward's Hospital and details are given in captions 76 to 83.

71. This is Leek Brook East Junction in about 1905, with NSR 0-6-0T no. 135 plus an inspection train. The curve towards Leek is on the right. (R.Humm coll.)

72. The curved Leek Brook platform, on the line to Stoke-on-Trent, is seen from a train running from there to Leek on 4th September 1954. Workers at Wardle's factory in the background were also allowed to use this stop. (H.C.Casserley)

73. Junction Box is seen again as an SLS railtour runs north towards Leek. Carrying BR no. 50703, but showing LMS on its tank, the 2-4-2T has just run through Cheddleton. (Colour-Rail.com)

74. The same location is seen from the signal box steps on 4th September 1973. No. D5285 is probably propelling the van to attach it to a sand train. This was authorised in those days. By 2017, a single line ran under the train and went on to curve right, almost to Ipstones. There were also very short lengths towards Leek, top left, and towards Stoke, lower left. Both had prospects of future extensions. (Colour-Rail.com)

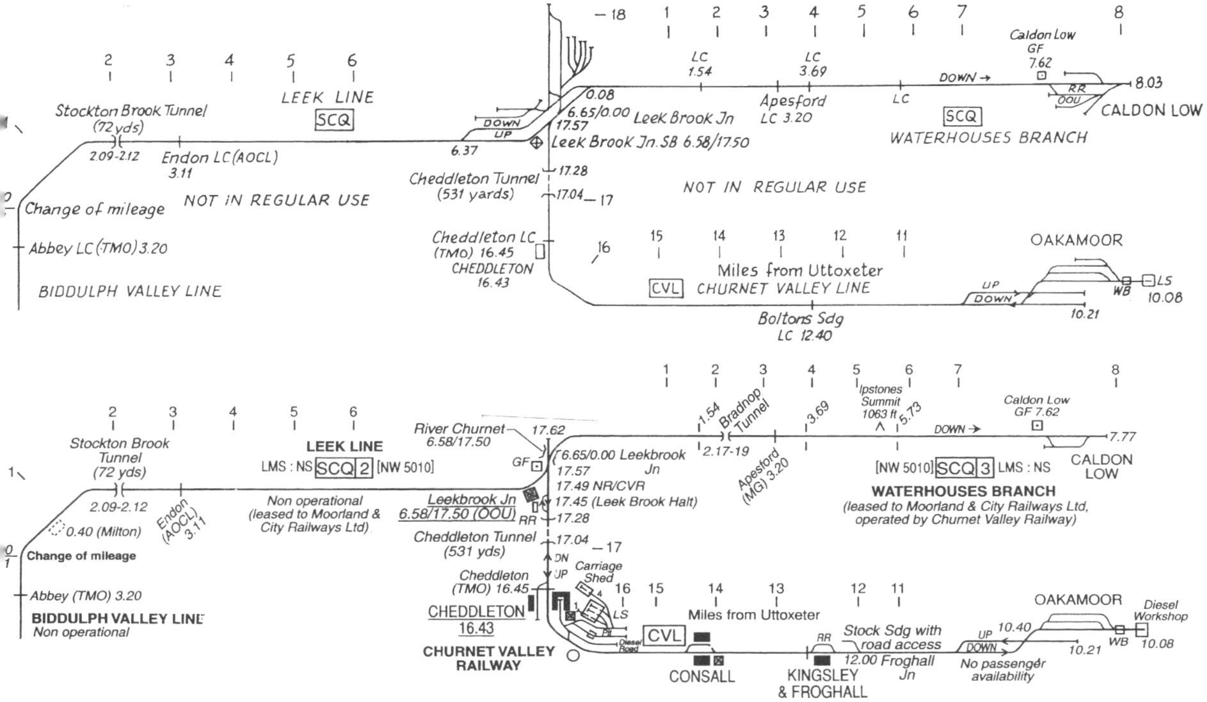

Top diagram labels (1990):

LEEK LINE — SCQ — Stockton Brook Tunnel (72 yds) 2 3 4 5 6 — 2.09-2.12 — Endon LC (AOCL) 3.11 — NOT IN REGULAR USE

− 18 1 2 3 4 5 6 7 8 — LC 1.54 — LC 3.69 — Apesford LC 3.20 — LC — Caldon Low GF 7.62 — DOWN → — RR OOU — 8.03 CALDON LOW — SCQ — WATERHOUSES BRANCH

0.08 — 6.65/0.00 Leek Brook Jn — 17.57 — Leek Brook Jn.SB 6.58/1750 — 6.37 — DOWN UP

Change of mileage — Abbey LC (TMO) 3.20 — BIDDULPH VALLEY LINE

Cheddleton Tunnel (531 yards) — 17.28 — 17.04 — 17 — NOT IN REGULAR USE

Cheddleton LC (TMO) 16.45 — CHEDDLETON 16.43 — 16 — 15 14 13 12 11 — Miles from Uttoxeter — CVL — CHURNET VALLEY LINE — OAKAMOOR — UP DOWN — WB — LS 10.08 — 10.21

Boltons Sdg LC 12.40

Bottom diagram labels (2013):

Stockton Brook Tunnel (72 yds) 2 3 4 5 6 — 2.09-2.12 — Endon (AOCL) 3.11 — 0.40 (Milton) — LEEK LINE LMS : NS SCQ 2 [NW 5010] — Non operational (leased to Moorland & City Railways Ltd)

1 2 3 4 5 6 7 8 — 1.54 — Bradnop Tunnel — 2.17-19 — 3.69 — Ipstones Summit 1063 ft — 5.73 — Apesford (MG) 3.20 — Caldon Low GF 7.62 — DOWN → — 7.77 — CALDON LOW — [NW 5010] SCQ 3 LMS : NS — WATERHOUSES BRANCH (leased to Moorland & City Railways Ltd, operated by Churnet Valley Railway)

River Churnet 17.62 6.58/17.50 — GF — 6.65/0.00 Leekbrook Jn — 17.57 — 17.49 NR/CVR — 17.45 (Leek Brook Halt) — RR — 17.28 — Leekbrook Jn 6.58/17.50 (OOU)

Change of mileage — Abbey (TMO) 3.20 — BIDDULPH VALLEY LINE Non operational

Cheddleton Tunnel (531 yards) — 17.04 — 17 — DN UP — Carriage Shed — Cheddleton (TMO) 16.45 — CHEDDLETON 16.43 — CHURNET VALLEY RAILWAY — Diesel Road — LS — 16 15 14 13 12 11 — Miles from Uttoxeter — CVL — CONSALL — RR — Stock Sdg with road access — 12.00 Froghall — KINGSLEY & FROGHALL — Froghall Jn — No passenger availability — OAKAMOOR — Diesel Workshop — UP DOWN 10.40 — 10.21 — WB 10.08

XVIII. The top diagram is from 1990 and reveals the revised layout which allowed reversal of trains running between the Churnet Valley and the Biddulph Valley. Below is the 2013 arrangement, with a loop provided south of the signal box. While it is shown as out of use, it became a visitor centre. (© TRACK maps)

75. No. 40174 arrives at Leek Brook Junction on 10th April 1984 with the second portion of the day's Caldon Low to Witton limestone train, comprising MSV and MTV former iron-ore tippler wagons. The two tracks on the left are dead-end sidings; the branch to Oakamoor is just out of sight behind Junction Box. The line from Leek was single from 1st January 1968. The 1867 box housed a 40-lever frame and was last manned on 14th June 1989. (P.D.Shannon)

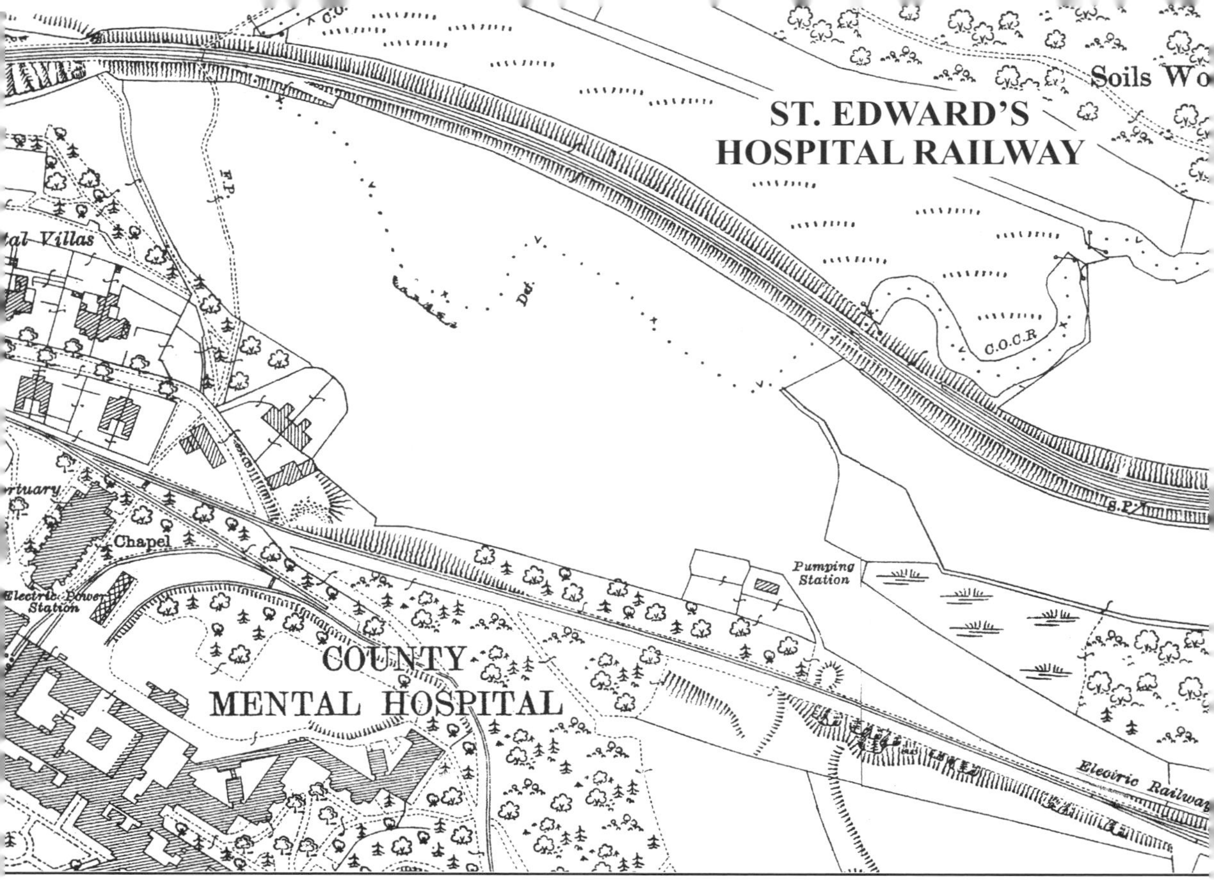

ST. EDWARD'S
HOSPITAL RAILWAY

Soils Wo

al Villas

rtuary

Chapel

Electric Power
Station

COUNTY
MENTAL HOSPITAL

Pumping
Station

S.P.

Electric Railway

C.O.C.R.

XIX.   The tracks on the right continue from those on the left of map XVII, albeit with a slight gap.

76.   A view north, taken from the track from Leek, reveals that it had no platform for trains from there, only to it. The hospital train ran on 200 volts DC, its source being shown on the left of map XIX. (T&LRS)

77. Leek Brook Halt was provided for workmen and hospital passengers only, but it did appear once in *Bradshaw's Guide*, in January 1929. It was in use from July 1904 until 31st October 1954. (T&LRS)

78. A view towards Cheddleton Tunnel shows the first curve on the line and the balanced overhead conductor system. There is a second track shown on the right of map XIX. (T&LRS)

79. Loaded coal wagons were propelled towards the hospital by its locomotive, having been shunted onto its branch by a main line engine. It is starting its journey, with Wardle's factory being in the background. (T&LRS)

80. The locomotive had controls at both ends and the driver could see over coal wagons. The small tram used for visitors would be hauled usually, but its use lasted only until the 1920s. (T&LRS)

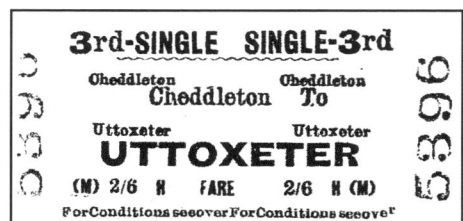

81. The line was ¾ mile in length and had a maximum gradient of 1 in 16.6, near the hospital; a test on the mentality of some, no doubt. The hospital closed in 2001 and much of it was converted to dwellings. (T&LRS)

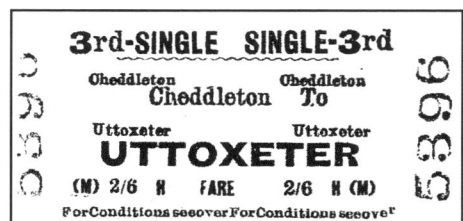

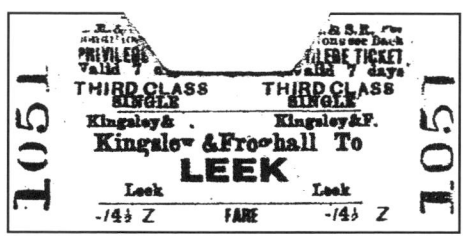

82. The end of the route is in sight and the source of water for the boilers becomes evident. Much coal would be stored in the open and, thus, have to be shovelled twice. After closure, the water tower was adapted for residential use, with splendid views. (T&LRS)

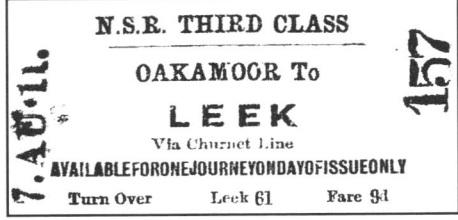

N.S.R. THIRD CLASS

OAKAMOOR To

LEEK

Via Churnet Line

AVAILABLE FOR ONE JOURNEY ON DAY OF ISSUE ONLY

Turn Over   Leek 61   Fare 9d

7.AU.11.

157

83. Wagons became national property during World War II and so, when boards were repaired, no attempts were made to restore lettering. The hand brake is to the right of the open door. The locomotive's doorway changed shape during its life. 'SC' stood for Stephenson Clarke. (T&LRS)

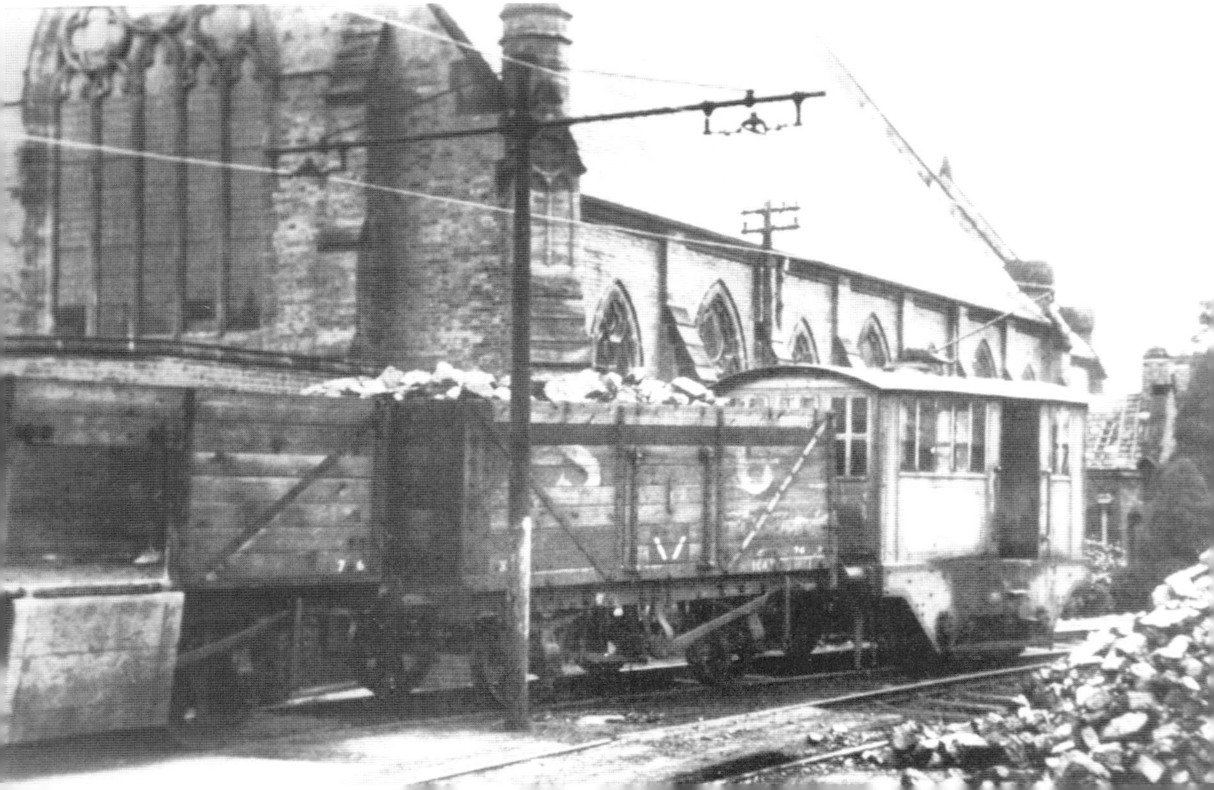

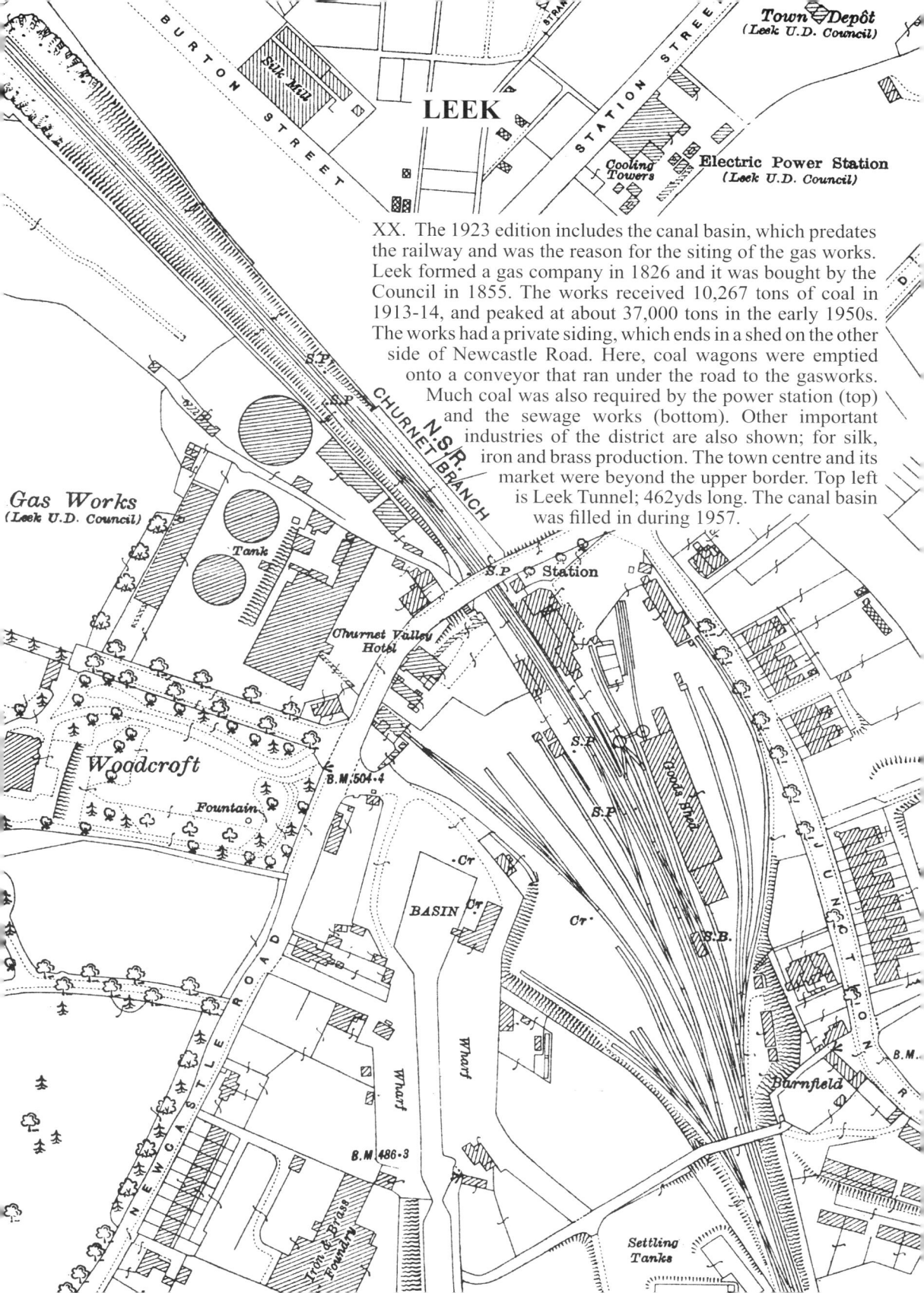

Town Depôt
(Leek U.D. Council)

LEEK

Cooling Towers | **Electric Power Station**
(Leek U.D. Council)

BURTON STREET

Silk Mill

STATION STREET

XX. The 1923 edition includes the canal basin, which predates the railway and was the reason for the siting of the gas works. Leek formed a gas company in 1826 and it was bought by the Council in 1855. The works received 10,267 tons of coal in 1913-14, and peaked at about 37,000 tons in the early 1950s. The works had a private siding, which ends in a shed on the other side of Newcastle Road. Here, coal wagons were emptied onto a conveyor that ran under the road to the gasworks. Much coal was also required by the power station (top) and the sewage works (bottom). Other important industries of the district are also shown; for silk, iron and brass production. The town centre and its market were beyond the upper border. Top left is Leek Tunnel; 462yds long. The canal basin was filled in during 1957.

N.S.R. CHURNET BRANCH

S.P.

Gas Works
(Leek U.D. Council)

Tank

S.P. ◇ Station

Churnet Valley Hotel

Woodcroft

B.M.504·4

Fountain

S.P.

Goods Shed

S.P.

·Cr·

S.B.

BASIN Cr·

Cr·

JUNCTION

B.M.

Barnfield

Wharf

Wharf

B.M.486·3

NEWCASTLE ROAD

Iron & Brass Foundry

Settling Tanks

84.   The extensive goods shed is beyond the bay platform in the distance. Out of view are its two turntables, which facilitated manual or horse movements of wagons and vans. (J.Alsop coll.)

Other views of this station can be found in pictures 2 to 10 in *Branch Line from Leek* **(Middleton Press).**

85.   This view in the other direction, also from about 1900, includes the platform drop at the barrow crossing. The northern part was a late addition. Many parcels, boxes and churns had to change trains here, demanding numerous barrow movements. Passengers also used the foot crossings, until a bridge came, shortly before closure. (P.Laming coll.)

86.   It is 19th August 1933 and no. 2364 is departing south with a mixture of coaches. It is a class 4P 2-6-4T. The nearest parts of both goods yards had been added in 1913-14, after the road bridge had been lengthened. Also in the way was the 1880 engine shed, which had been lower left. The replacement was built at Leek Brook Junction. (R.Humm coll.)

87.   The prospective passenger's perspective was on the town side of the station and is seen on 11th April 1955, with a Morris Minor in attendance. The growth of motoring was about to start. A supermarket now occupies the site. (R.Humm coll.)

88. No. 42603 is a class 4MT 2-6-4T and it is seen from the southern barrow crossing in 1962. Passenger service ended on 6th January 1964. The final steam special ran on 2nd January 1965. The goods yard would close on 6th July 1970 and the shed was demolished in 1979. (Colour-Rail.com)

89. Recorded on 27th January 1962 is another 4MT, this time no. 42668. This successful class was noted for good performance and this one is working the 1.35pm to Stoke-on-Trent. On the right is the 40-lever signal box, which was in use from May 1914 until 31st December 1967. (Colour-Rail.com)

RUDYARD LAKE

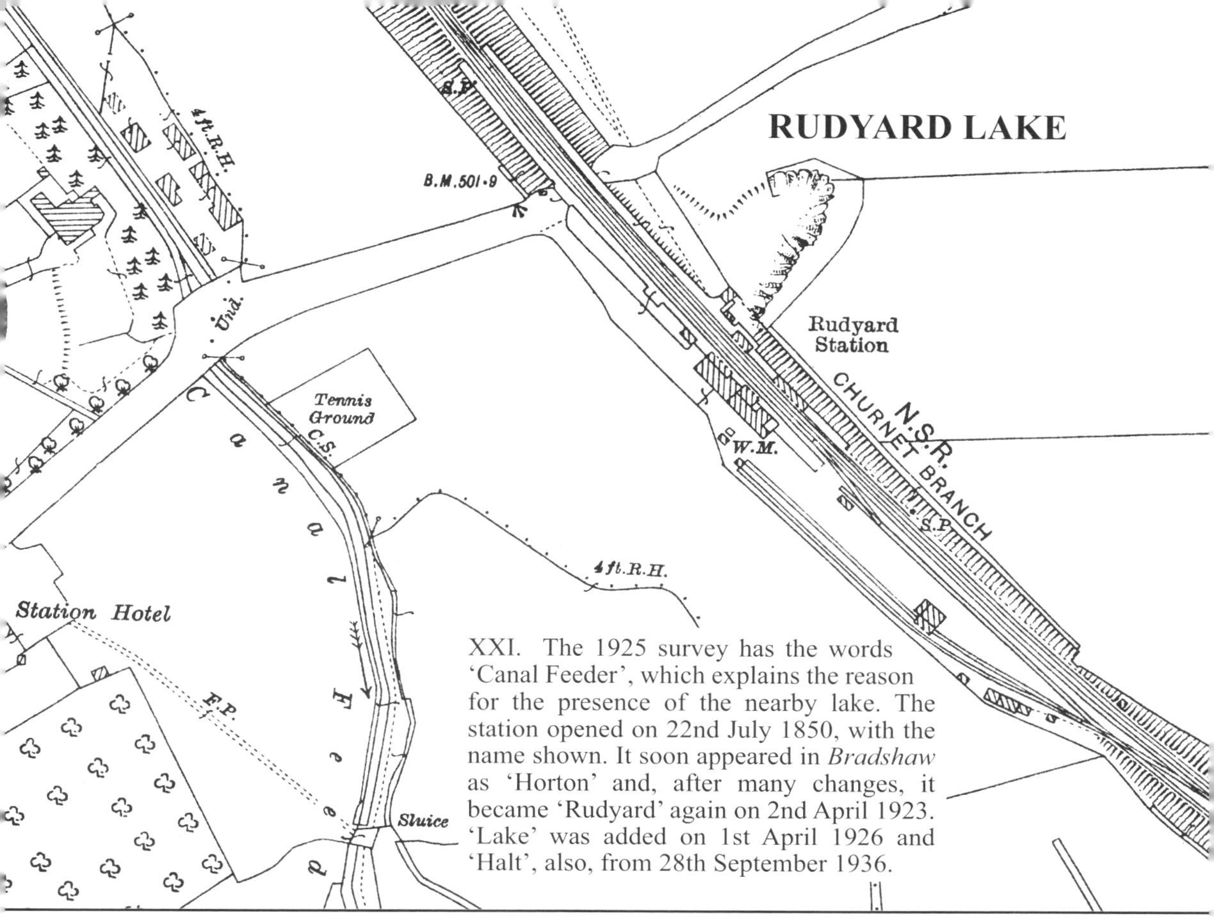

Rudyard Station
N.S.R.
CHURNET BRANCH
Tennis Ground
Station Hotel
Sluice
C a n a l F e e d
4ft.R.H.
B.M.501·9
W.M.
S.P.
F.P.
C.S.
Und.

XXI. The 1925 survey has the words 'Canal Feeder', which explains the reason for the presence of the nearby lake. The station opened on 22nd July 1850, with the name shown. It soon appeared in *Bradshaw* as 'Horton' and, after many changes, it became 'Rudyard' again on 2nd April 1923. 'Lake' was added on 1st April 1926 and 'Halt', also, from 28th September 1936.

90. The dam that created the lake was completed in 1797. It has been in use ever since. A tank engine in NSR livery passes the structure in about 1900. Visitors have continued to come to sail, row, fish and walk. A promenade was ready in 1876 and a roller-skating rink was added by then. A bandstand followed, as did a dance floor. (J.Alsop coll.)

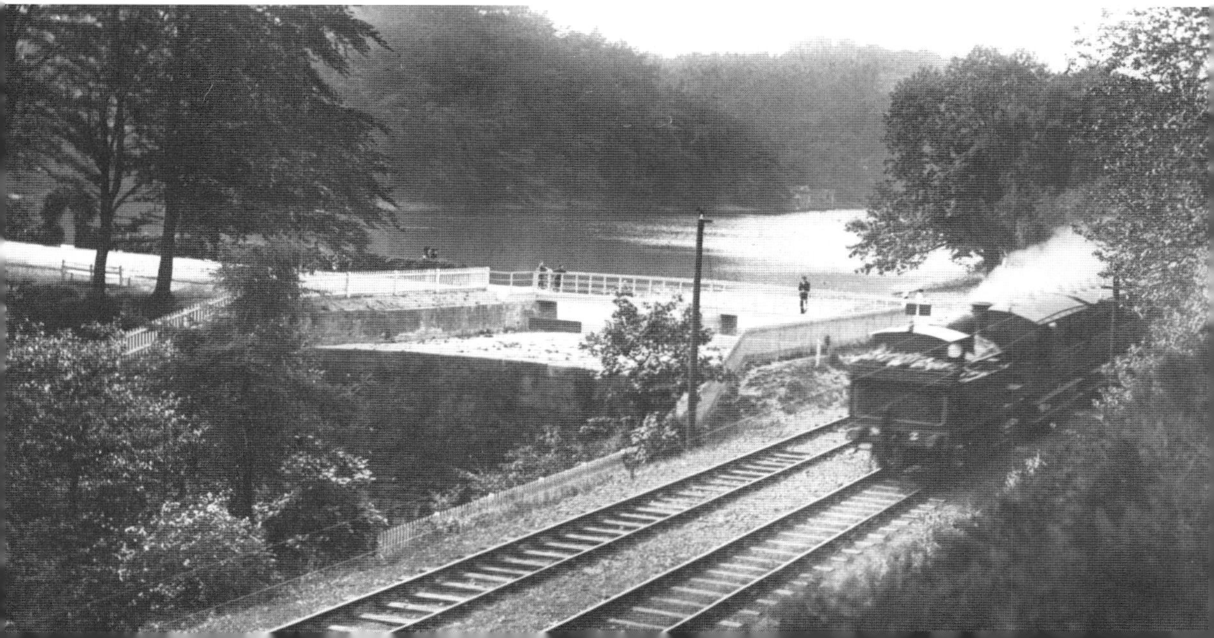

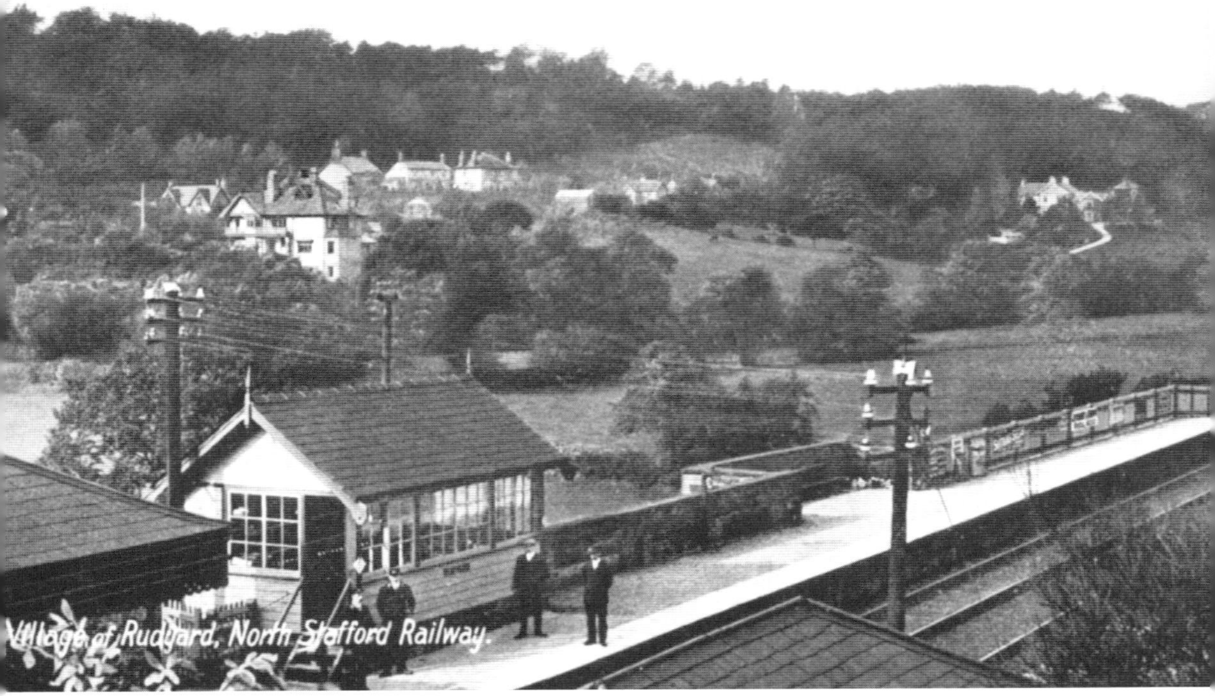
Village of Rudyard, North Stafford Railway.

91. Part of the village is included. Its census in 1901 revealed 81 residents. There had recently been over 50,000 visitors annually. The dances often necessitated extra trains. The hotel was extended in 1883 and a floating landing stage arrived in 1906. Roundabouts and organs added to the attractions. The postcard was issued in about 1908. (J.Alsop coll.)

92. A record from 27th May 1953 confirms 'Rudyard Lake' on the LMS 'Hawkseye' sign on the left. The machine on the right offered chocolate bars to the crowds. The platforms had been lengthened in 1911, as excursion trains became longer. (J.Alsop coll.)

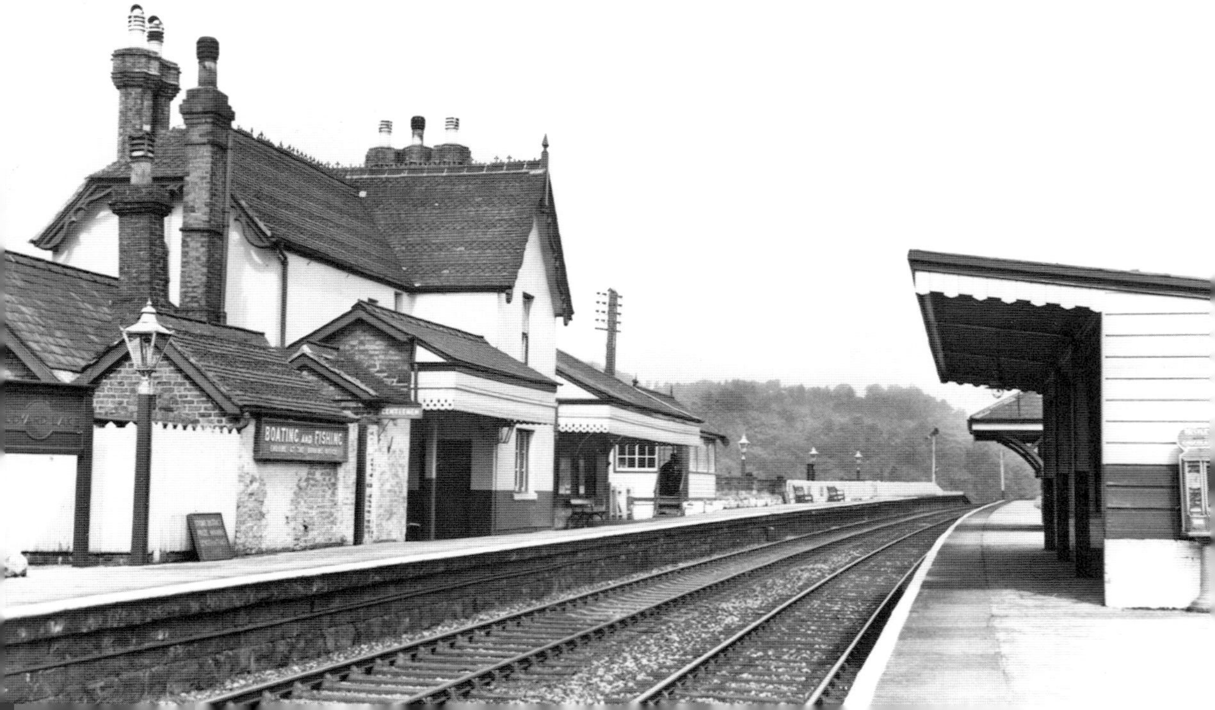
BOATING AND FISHING

93. The buildings were destroyed in 1970, having been closed on 7th November 1960. The goods yard was taken out of use on the same day. The signal box is still named 'Rudyard Station' in this view from about 1950. It contained 14 levers and functioned from 1909 to 19th November 1960. (SLS coll.)

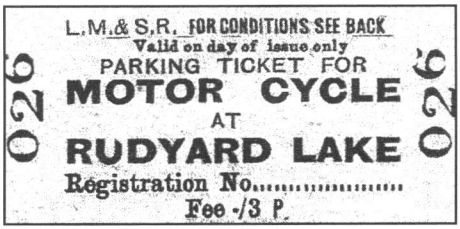

L.M.&S.R.   FOR CONDITIONS SEE BACK
Valid on day of issue only
PARKING TICKET FOR
MOTOR CAR or
THREE-WHEELED VEHICLE
AT
RUDYARD LAKE
Registration No.
Fee -/

063   063

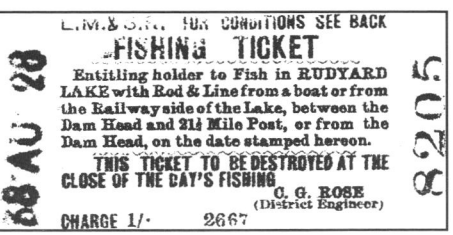

L.M.&S.R.   FOR CONDITIONS SEE BACK
FISHING TICKET
Entitling holder to Fish in RUDYARD LAKE with Rod & Line from a boat or from the Railway side of the Lake, between the Dam Head and 2½ Mile Post, or from the Dam Head, on the date stamped hereon.
THIS TICKET TO BE DESTROYED AT THE CLOSE OF THE DAY'S FISHING
C. G. ROSE
(District Engineer)
CHARGE 1/-   2667

28 AU 28   8205

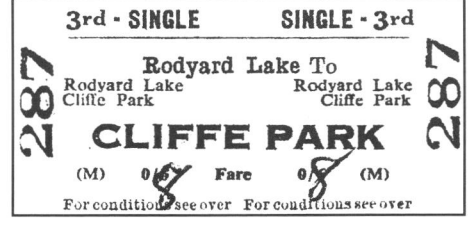

L.M.&S.R. FOR CONDITIONS SEE BACK
Valid on day of issue only
PARKING TICKET FOR
MOTOR CYCLE
AT
RUDYARD LAKE
Registration No.
Fee -/3 P

026   026

3rd - SINGLE   SINGLE - 3rd
Rodyard Lake To
Rodyard Lake   Rodyard Lake
Cliffe Park   Cliffe Park
CLIFFE PARK
(M)   0   Fare   0   (M)
For conditions see over   For conditions see over

287   287

LEEK & RUDYARD RAILWAY

94.   The first miniature railway here was of 10¼in gauge and was run during 1976-78. The engine was based on the 2-6-2T no.1 *E.R.Calthrop*, which worked in the Manifold Valley in 1905-34. The railway was rebuilt and reopened in 1985 and is seen on 20th September 1991 with Bo-Bo DM *Rudyard Lady* heading the 12.40 to Lakeside. This station was called Rudyard for Horton. The line had grown to 1½ miles in length. (A.Nicholls)

95.   A view from 2006 shows no. 7 *Merlin*, a 2-4-2T built in 1998 by the Exmoor Steam Railway for a line in West Germany. It arrived here in 2001. The name was part of the legend concerning King Arthur. (Colour-Rail.com)

96. Two photos from 5th August 2012 show the enlarged facilities at Rudyard station, with 2-4-2T no. 9 *Pendragon* running round. It was built in 1994 as *Ashorne* by the Exmoor Steam Railway and arrived here in 2006. (R.Humm)

97. A view from the footbridge features a train arriving behind no. 8 *King Arthur* 0-6-2T, which was built in 2005. The railway has changed ownership several times and most of the stock of the Isle of Mull Railway came here upon its closure in 2011. This included 1986 diesel *Glen Auldyn* and 2-6-2T *Victoria*, from Mouse Boiler Works in 1993. (R.Humm)

98.   The 2016 Steam Gala offered a fine display. From left to right: *Excalibur* 2-4-2T, built in 1993 (just behind is diesel locomotive, *Frances*, ex-Isle of Mull Railway); *Pendragon* 2-4-2T, built in 1994; visiting engine, *Nelly*, 2-4-0T, built as an 0-4-0 in 1977; *King Arthur* 0-6-2T, built in 2005; and *Waverley* 4-4-2T, built in 1948. The new owner's name is above the door and in brackets here. (Leek & Rudyard Railway)

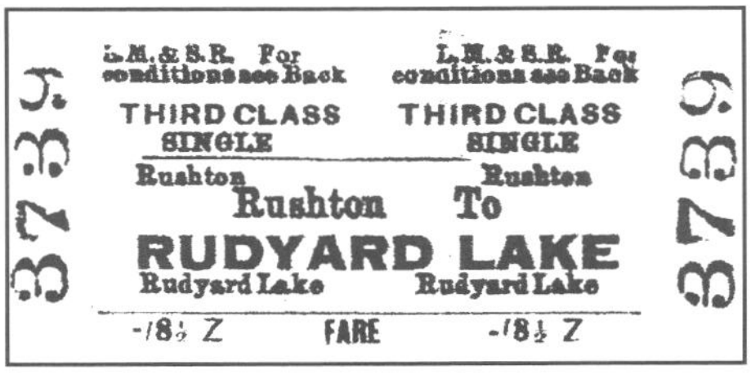

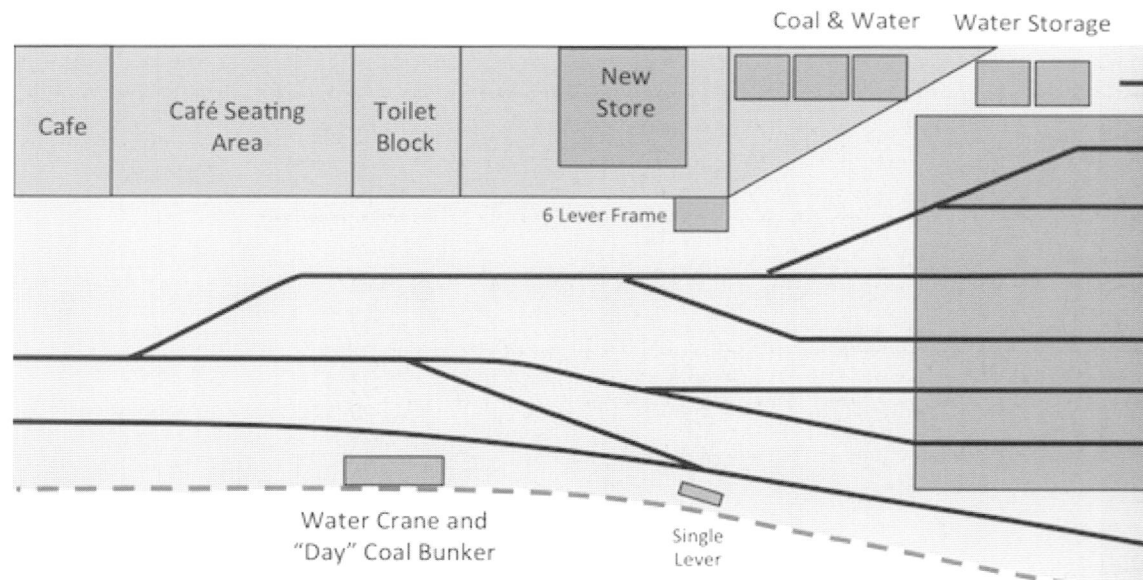

99.   We move to the other end of the line at Hunthouse Wood and witness 0-4-2T no. 8 *King Arthur* on 5th August 2012. An extensive part of the track bed of the NSR was eventually used by the miniature railway. A loop had been provided part way at Lakeside. (R.Humm)

Coal & Water   Water Storage

| Cafe | Café Seating Area | Toilet Block | New Store |

6 Lever Frame

Water Crane and "Day" Coal Bunker

Single Lever

Leek and Rudyard Railway
NO
PUBLIC
ACCESS

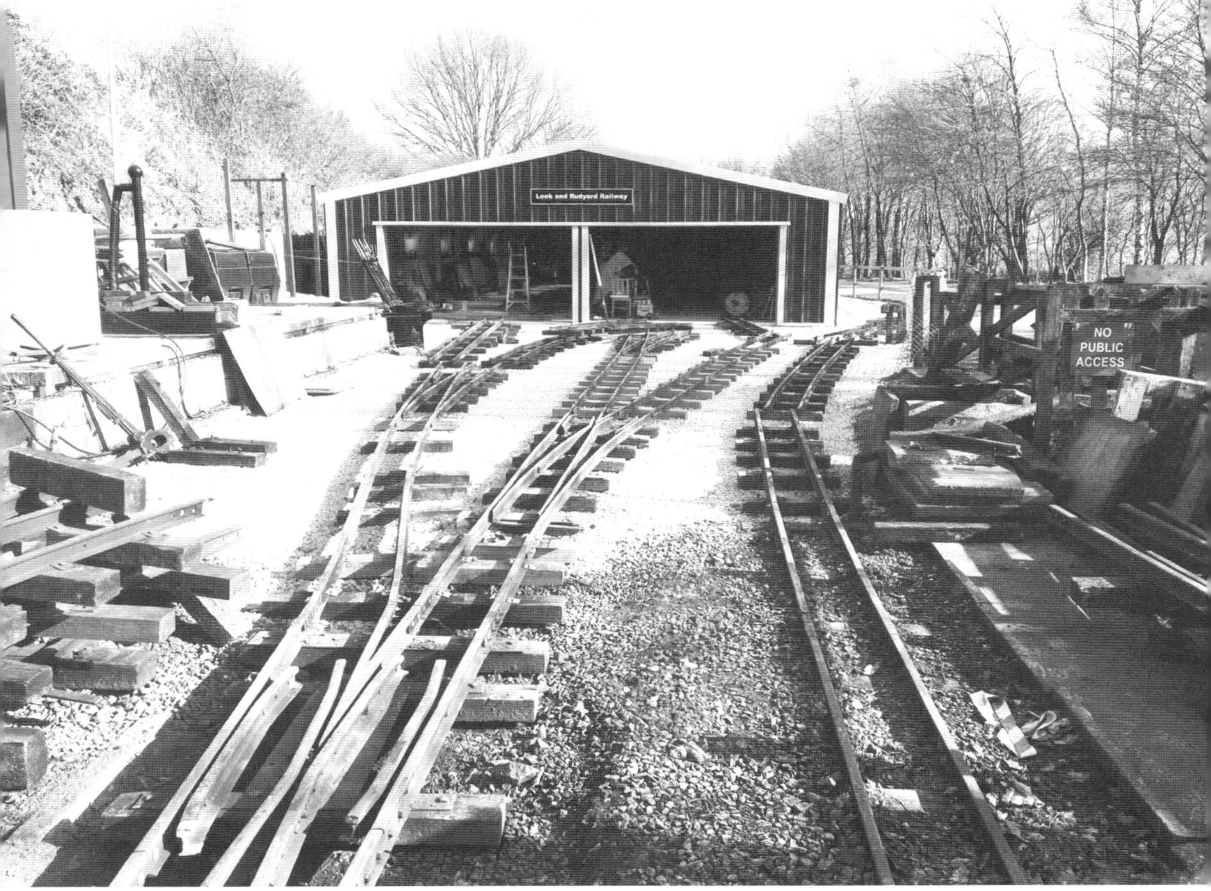

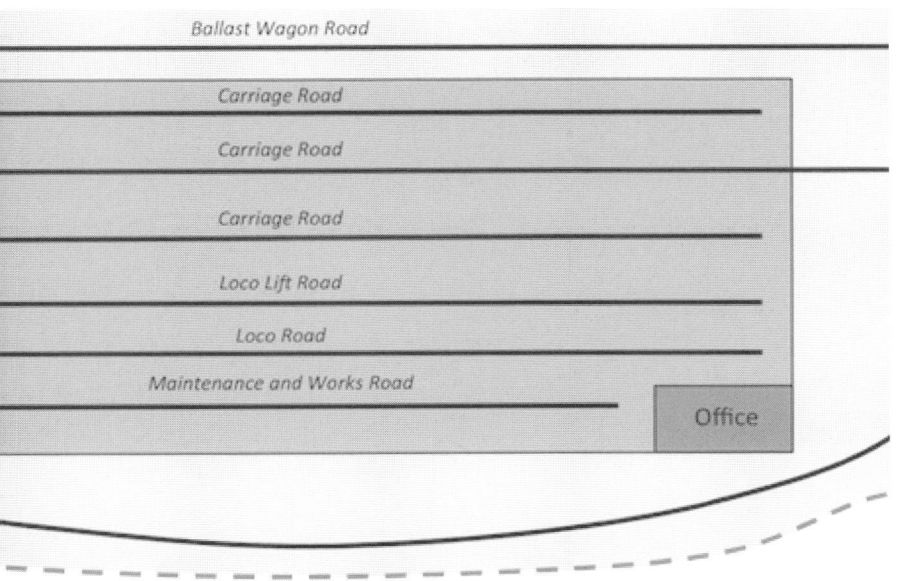

100. A further change of ownership in December 2015 brought plans for major improvements in several areas. A vast increase in engine shed dimensions and facilities resulted. Progress was recorded on 4th April 2017. (Leek & Rudyard Railway)

Ballast Wagon Road
Carriage Road
Carriage Road
Carriage Road
Loco Lift Road
Loco Road
Maintenance and Works Road
Office

XXII. The new layout, seen in April 2017, included track parts from the Isle of Mull Railway.

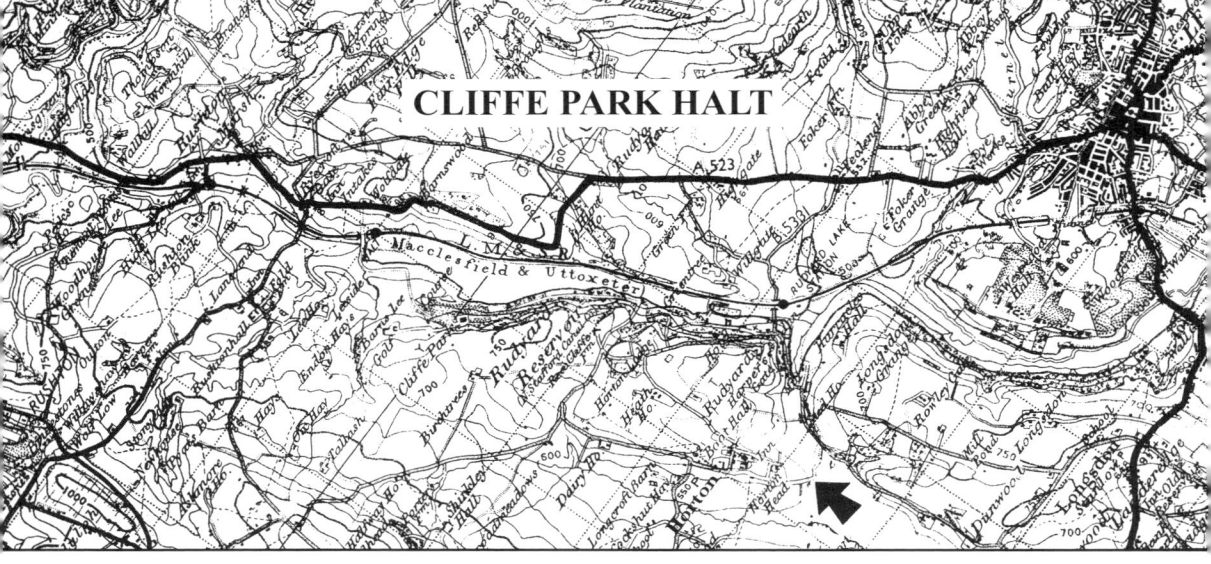

CLIFFE PARK HALT

XXIII. The 1947 map at 1in to 1 mile shows Leek top right and Leek Tunnel to the left of the station. The route name is set along the length of the Lake, which is correctly termed 'Rudyard Reservoir (N.Stafford Canal Co.)' nearby. Above these words are: Cliffe Park, Golf Course and HALT. Further north is Rushton and its station.

101. This stop opened on 1st May 1905 as 'Rudyard Lake', but it became 'Cliffe Park' on 1st April 1926. 'Halt' was added on 28th September 1936. Northbound in 1960 is 2-6-4T no. 42665. The lake extends for 2½ miles in total. The original shelter is the nearest one on the left platform. (A.Dudman coll.)

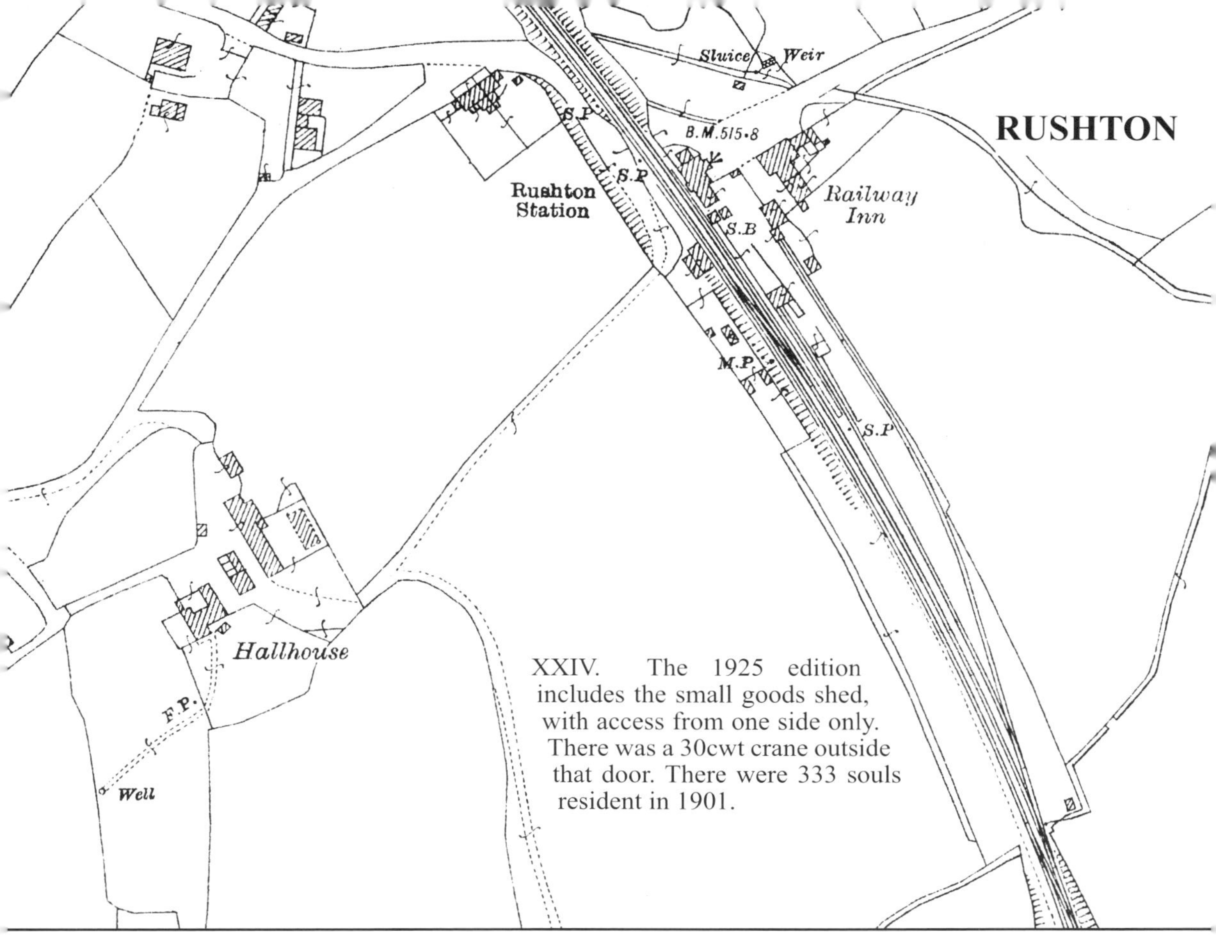

RUSHTON

Rushton Station

Railway Inn

Hallhouse

Well

XXIV.   The 1925 edition includes the small goods shed, with access from one side only. There was a 30cwt crane outside that door. There were 333 souls resident in 1901.

102. The proximity of the Railway Inn to the station becomes clear in this view from the west. Nearest are windows for the station master to use, when off duty. The upper ones in the next picture are likewise. (R.Humm coll.)

103. The east facade has the main entrance for passengers and is seen on 27th May 1953, when road traffic was still minimal. All services were withdrawn on 7th November 1960. (J.Alsop coll.)

104. South of here was a siding on the west side. It was used to load farm products and hold empty excursion stock. Class 4P 2-6-4T no. 42319 is southbound in about 1955. The 1883 original box had 19 levers and remained in use until 27th July 1964. The block instruments were in the booking office. (SLS coll.)

BOSLEY

XXV. The 1909 edition includes the 2ft 6ins gauge railway of Francis R. Thompstone & Sons Ltd, which carried grain to its mills. The northern one is inset, lower left. The NSR nearest siding ends close to the boundary fence, behind the signal box (S.B.). The River Dane runs north, close to the dots and dashes of the Cheshire county boundary. The tramway continued about ½ mile to its wharf on the Macclesfield Canal. The mills had started with copper and brass in the 1760s, but moved to silk and cotton, before working on corn. Inset top right is the canal wharf and the terminal loop.

Weir

Sl.

477
3.185

Higher Works

L.B

Sl.

B.M.
426·7

S.B.

Waterfall

Sl.

F.B.

S.P.

Dane Mills
(Corn)

Bosley Works Bridge

W.M.

Bosley
Station

S.P.

S.R.

Lock

T R A M W A Y

M.P.

Sl.

Tank

...ford
...dge

Lowerworks
Mill
(Corn)

Sl.

Harrington
House

W.

S.D.

Uni...

105. Thompstone's Bagnall 0-4-0 *Magnet I* is seen hauling bags of corn. It was used from 1887 until 1909, when it was replaced by *Magnet II*, a similar unit. Closure came around 1925. The works was subsequently used for the treatment of wood chips, until destroyed in three massive explosions in 2015, involving four fatalities. (A.Dudman coll.)

106. The northern facade of the main building is featured here, along with the sloping fencing seen in the next picture. Local residents numbered 353 in 1901 and 413 in 1961. (R.Humm coll.)

107. The station buildings largely obscure the mills. The 22-lever signal box had a gate wheel and came into use in 1901. Closure came on 27th July 1964. (J.Alsop coll.)

108. The lengthy goods shed and shelter are on the fringe of this and the previous picture. Class 4P 2-6-4T no. 42575 is seen with a stopping train bound for Leek, in the early 1950s. The station site has now been obliterated by industrial premises. (SLS)

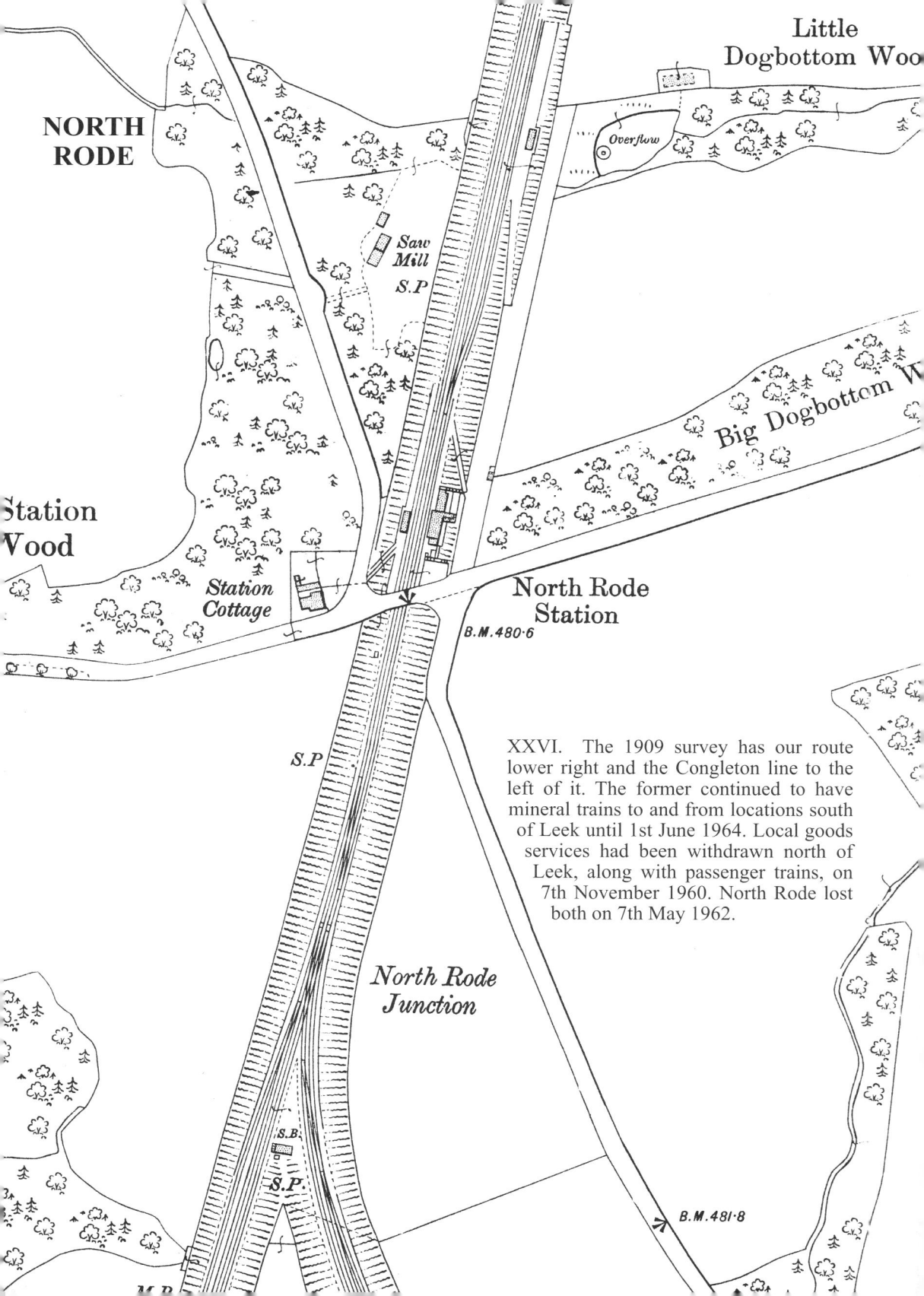

NORTH RODE

Little
Dogbottom Woo

Overflow

Saw
Mill
S.P

Big Dogbottom W

Station
Wood

Station
Cottage

North Rode
Station

B.M. 480·6

S.P

XXVI. The 1909 survey has our route lower right and the Congleton line to the left of it. The former continued to have mineral trains to and from locations south of Leek until 1st June 1964. Local goods services had been withdrawn north of Leek, along with passenger trains, on 7th November 1960. North Rode lost both on 7th May 1962.

North Rode
Junction

B.M. 481·8

S.B.

S.P.

109. The single siding is in the distance, on the right, in this panorama from 29th May 1950. Local residents numbered 276 in 1901. Diamond lattice brickwork was a lavish feature on the main elevation. There were milk churn slides down to both platforms. (J.Alsop coll.)

110. The map shows the orientation of the signal box at the junction. Track lifting towards Bosley began here in July 1964. The box had 30 levers and was used from 1869 until 21st March 1965. Upon closure, the down siding was converted to a Down Goods Loop, which lasted until 1969. The crossover was retained, worked from North Rode Ground Frame, which was finally abolished in 1991. (R.Humm coll.)

111. The box is in the distance on 15th September 1956 as ex-LMS 'Rebuilt Patriot' class 4-6-0 no. 45530 *Sir Frank Ree* heads the down 'Comet'.
(R.Humm coll.)

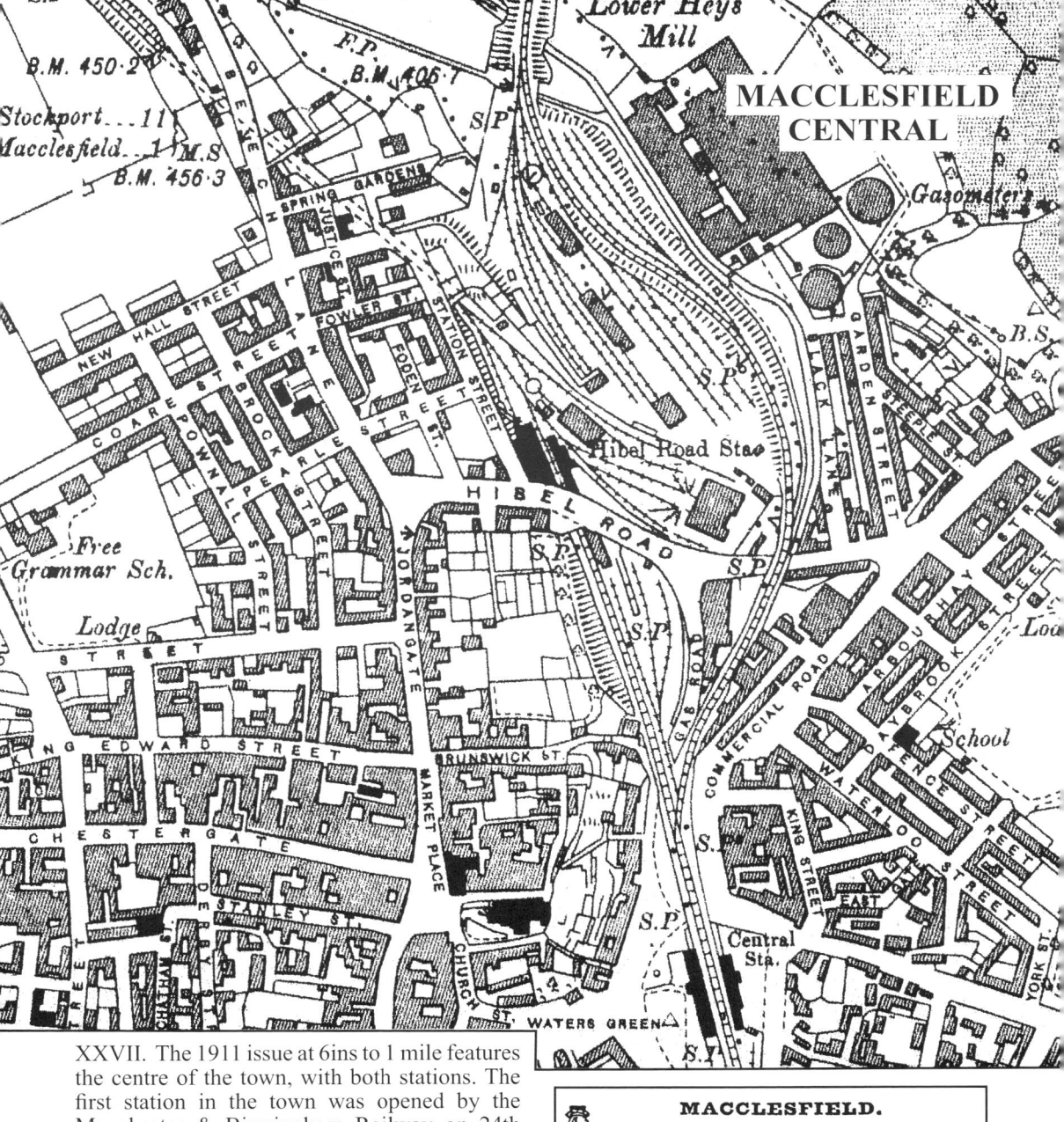

XXVII. The 1911 issue at 6ins to 1 mile features the centre of the town, with both stations. The first station in the town was opened by the Manchester & Birmingham Railway on 24th November 1845. It was north of the tunnel, which is top left on the map. It was a terminus until 18th June 1849, when it closed and Hibel Road opened. We will dwell at Central, although most of the trains from Leek terminated at Hibel Road. That station closed to passengers on 7th November 1960 and to goods on 3rd November 1962. Top centre is the route north to Marple, which was in use from 1869 to 1970.

Extract from *Bradshaw's Guide 1866*, as seen on TV. (Reprinted by Middleton Press)

MACCLESFIELD.

A telegraph station.
HOTELS.—Macclesfield Arms, Angel.
MARKET DAYS.—Tuesdays and Saturdays.
FAIRS.—May 6, June 22, July 11, October 4, November 11.
BANKERS.—Brocklehurst and Co.; Branch of the Manchester and Liverpool District Banking Co.

A market town and borough, population, 36,101, who return two members. *St. Michael's Church* restored, with tombs of Archbishop Savage and the Leghs of Lyme, and *Christ Church*, with the tomb of Roe, its founder, are worth visiting. The *Town Hall*, by Godwin, *Free Grammar School, School of Design,* and *Public Park,* and the silk and cotton factories should be viewed.

112. This is the west elevation in about 1900 and, in the foreground, is Waters Green. Mills are evident in the town and the Peak District enhances the background. (J.Alsop coll.)

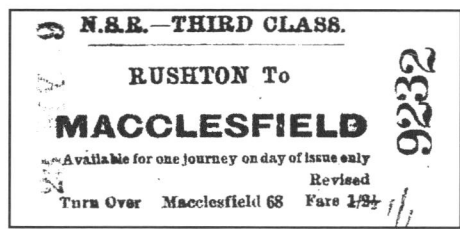

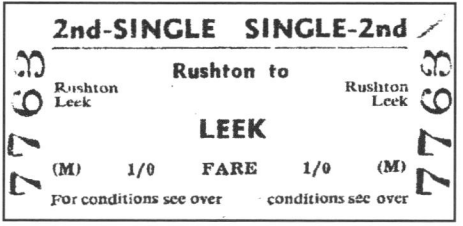

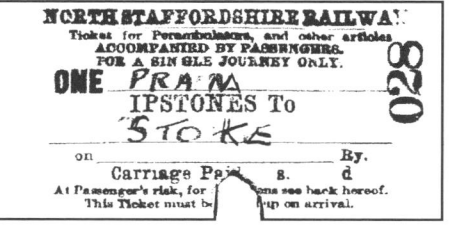

113. NSR no. 88 has generated an impressive start to the final section. The 0-6-0 was renumbered 8683 in 1928. The two-tone coaches add to the appeal of the system. (R.M.Casserley coll.)

114. No. 67451 is a class C14 4-4-2T, a type introduced in 1907, by the Great Central Railway. There were only 12 listed by 1948. To the south were Macclesfield Moss Box (20 levers) and Sutton Crossing Box (18 levers). Both closed on 21st March 1965. (R.Humm coll.)

115. Class C14 4-4-2T no. 67447 is standing on 18th April 1954 with the 11.0am (SuO) to Manchester. It is adorned with the BR logo, which appears to be a lion on a monocycle. (H.C.Casserley)

Table 129 — MANCHESTER, MACCLESFIELD, LEEK and UTTOXETER

A Saturdays only. Runs 27th June to 29th August inclusive
a Runs 26th July to 16th August inclusive
B Heaton Chapel and Heaton Moor
b Runs 28th June to 6th September
C Change at North Rode
C Saturdays only. Not after 29th August
C Dep Manchester (London Road) 12 20 and Stockport (Edgeley) 12 28 pm on Saturdays
D Arr 9 58 am on Mondays 22nd June to 31st Aug
E, E or £ Except Saturdays
F Fridays only. Runs 26th June to 28th August inclusive
f Fridays only. Mayfield Station on Fridays
H Does not run 20th June and 12th September
H Every hour 10 14 am to 9 14 pm
J Saturdays only. Runs 25th July to 15th August inclusive
J Dep 5 22 pm on Saturdays
K Fridays and Saturdays
L Saturdays only. Runs 26th June to 1st August inclusive
L From Hazel Grove dep 7 56 am
M Mondays only
N Saturdays only. Runs 1st to 22nd August inclusive
N Mayfield Station

P Saturdays only. Runs 18th July to 8th August inclusive
P Arr Stockport (Edgeley) 8 15 and Manchester (Mayfield) 8 24 am on Saturdays
R Saturdays only. Not after 5th September
R Arr 7 39 pm on 20th June 5th and 12th September
S, S or £ Saturdays only
T Saturdays only. Runs 4th July to 29th August inclusive
T Every hour 9 45 am to 8 45 pm
t Change at Macclesfield (Central)
U Wednesdays and Saturdays
U Mayfield Station on Saturdays
V 4 minutes later on Mondays
V Victoria Station
W Wednesdays only
X Except Mondays
X Except Fridays
Y Saturdays only. Runs 27th June to 5th September inclusive
Z Saturdays only. Runs 11th July to 29th August inclusive
‡ Dep 7 2 am on Saturdays, 4th July to 5th September
§ Via Derby. Extra fare
¶ Saturdays only. Commences 4th July

July 1960

116. A panorama from the same day gives an opportunity to appreciate the generous weather protection provided at this altitude. We are almost at 500ft above sea level. (H.C.Casserley)

117. It is 4th September 1954 and we see yet another class C14 4-4-2T. It is no. 67440, arriving with the 12.56pm from Manchester London Road. The through lines have been modernised with flat bottom rails. (R.M.Casserley)

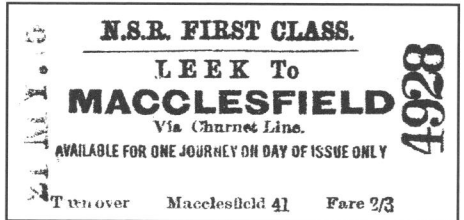

118. The 1933 box is seen. It had 50 levers and was in use until 19th December 1965. Its replacement had 55 levers and was still working in 2017. It was built east of the running lines. (Colour-Rail.com)

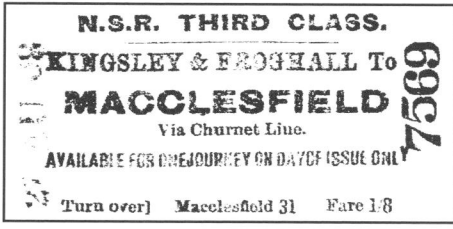

119. This photograph is from almost the same viewpoint and was taken on 11th June 1957. The Marple line curves to the right, near the rear of the DMU. The route had been a joint line-NSR/GCR, until 1923. (Colour-Rail.com)

120. The term 'Central' was dropped on 11th September 1961, ten months after Hibel Road had closed. The Cheadle Hulme to Macclesfield section was energised on 26th April 1965 and four-car units were introduced on 14th June 1965 to Manchester Piccadilly. Wiring south to Stoke-on-Trent allowed electric traction from 6th March 1967. (H.C.Casserley)

MP Middleton Press
EVOLVING THE ULTIMATE RAIL ENCYCLOPEDIA
Easebourne Midhurst GU29 9AZ. Tel:01730 813169
www.middletonpress.co.uk email:info@middletonpress.co.uk
A-978 0 906520 B- 978 1 873793 C- 978 1 901706 D-978 1 904474
E - 978 1 906008 F - 978 1 908174 G - 978 1 910356

All titles listed below were in print at time of publication - please check current availability by looking at our website - *www.middletonpress.co.uk* or by requesting a Brochure which includes our *LATEST* RAILWAY TITLES also our TRAMWAY, TROLLEYBUS, MILITARY and COASTAL series

A
Abergavenny to Merthyr C 91 8
Abertillery & Ebbw Vale Lines D 84 5
Aberystwyth to Carmarthen E 90 1
Allhallows - Branch Line to A 62 8
Alton - Branch Lines to A 11 6
Andover to Southampton A 82 6
Ascot - Branch Lines around A 64 2
Ashburton - Branch Line to B 95 4
Ashford - Steam to Eurostar B 67 1
Ashford to Dover A 48 2
Austrian Narrow Gauge D 04 3
Avonmouth - BL around D 42 5
Aylesbury to Rugby D 91 3
B
Baker Street to Uxbridge D 90 6
Bala to Llandudno E 87 1
Banbury to Birmingham D 27 2
Banbury to Cheltenham E 63 5
Bangor to Holyhead F 01 7
Bangor to Portmadoc E 72 7
Barking to Southend C 80 2
Barmouth to Pwllheli E 53 6
Barry - Branch Lines around D 50 0
Bartlow - Branch Lines to F 27 7
Bath Green Park to Bristol C 36 9
Bath to Evercreech Junction A 60 4
Beamish 40 years on rails E94 9
Bedford to Wellingborough D 31 9
Berwick to Drem F 64 2
Berwick to St. Boswells F 75 8
B'ham to Tamworth & Nuneaton F 63 5
Birkenhead to West Kirby F 61 1
Birmingham to Wolverhampton E253
Blackburn to Hellifield F 95 6
Bletchley to Cambridge D 94 4
Bletchley to Rugby E 07 9
Bodmin - Branch Lines around B 83 1
Boston to Lincoln F 80 2
Bournemouth to Evercreech Jn A 46 8
Bournemouth to Weymouth A 57 4
Bradshaw's History F18 5
Bradshaw's Rail Times 1850 F 13 0
Bradshaw's Rail Times 1895 F 11 6
Branch Lines series - see town names
Brecon to Neath D 43 2
Brecon to Newport D 16 6
Brecon to Newtown E 06 2
Brighton to Eastbourne A 16 1
Brighton to Worthing A 03 1
Bristol to Taunton D 03 6
Bromley South to Rochester B 23 7
Bromsgrove to Birmingham D 87 6
Bromsgrove to Gloucester D 73 9
Broxbourne to Cambridge F16 1
Brunel - A railtour D 74 6
Bude - Branch Line to B 29 9
Burnham to Evercreech Jn B 68 0
C
Cambridge to Ely D 55 5
Canterbury - BLs around B 58 9
Cardiff to Dowlais (Cae Harris) E 47 5
Cardiff to Pontypridd E 95 6
Cardiff to Swansea E 42 0
Carlisle to Hawick E 85 7
Carmarthen to Fishguard E 66 6
Caterham & Tattenham Corner B251
Central & Southern Spain NG E 91 8
Chard and Yeovil - BLs a C 30 7
Charing Cross to Dartford A 75 8
Charing Cross to Orpington A 96 3
Cheddar - Branch Line to B 90 9
Cheltenham to Andover C 43 7
Cheltenham to Redditch D 81 4
Chester to Birkenhead F 21 5
Chester to Manchester F 51 2
Chester to Rhyl E 93 2
Chester to Warrington F 40 6
Chichester to Portsmouth A 14 7
Clacton and Walton - BLs to F 04 8
Clapham Jn to Beckenham Jn B 36 7
Cleobury Mortimer - BLs a E 18 5
Clevedon & Portishead - BLs to D180
Consett to South Shields E 57 4
Cornwall Narrow Gauge D 56 2
Corris and Vale of Rheidol E 65 9
Coventry to Leicester G 00 5
Craven Arms to Llandeilo E 35 2
Craven Arms to Wellington E 33 8
Crawley to Littlehampton A 34 5
Crewe to Manchester F 57 4
Cromer - Branch Lines around C 26 0
Croydon to East Grinstead B 48 0
Crystal Palace & Catford Loop B 87 1
Cyprus Narrow Gauge E 13 0
D
Darjeeling Revisited F 09 3
Darlington Leamside Newcastle E 28 4
Darlington to Newcastle D 98 2
Dartford to Sittingbourne B 34 3
Denbigh - Branch Lines around F 32 1
Derby to Stoke-on-Trent F 93 2
Derwent Valley - BL to the D 06 7
Devon Narrow Gauge E 09 3
Didcot to Banbury D 02 9
Didcot to Swindon C 84 0
Didcot to Winchester C 13 0
Dorset & Somerset NG D 76 0
Douglas - Laxey - Ramsey E 75 8
Douglas to Peel C 88 8
Douglas to Port Erin C 55 0
Douglas to Ramsey D 39 5
Dover to Ramsgate A 78 9
Drem to Edinburgh G 06 7
Dublin Northwards in 1950s E 31 4
Dunstable - Branch Lines to E 27 7
E
Ealing to Slough C 42 0
Eastbourne to Hastings A 27 7
East Cornwall Mineral Railways D 22 7
East Croydon to Three Bridges A 53 6
Eastern Spain Narrow Gauge E 56 7
East Grinstead - BLs to A 07 9
East Kent Light Railway A 61 1
East London - Branch Lines of C 44 4
East London Line B 80 0
East of Norwich - Branch Lines E 69 7
Effingham Junction - BLs a A 74 1
Ely to Norwich C 90 1
Enfield Town & Palace Gates D 32 6
Epsom to Horsham A 30 7
Eritrean Narrow Gauge E 38 3
Euston to Harrow & Wealdstone C 89 5
Exeter to Barnstaple B 15 2
Exeter to Newton Abbot C 49 9
Exeter to Tavistock B 69 5
Exmouth - Branch Lines to B 00 8
F
Fairford - Branch Line to A 52 9
Falmouth, Helston & St. Ives C 74 1
Fareham to Salisbury A 67 3
Faversham to Dover B 05 3
Felixstowe & Aldeburgh - BL to D 20 3
Fenchurch Street to Barking C 20 8
Festiniog - 50 yrs of enterprise C 83 3
Festiniog 1946-55 E 01 7
Festiniog in the Fifties B 68 8
Festiniog in the Sixties B 91 6
Ffestiniog in Colour 1955-82 F 25 3
Finsbury Park to Alexandra Pal C 02 8
French Metre Gauge Survivors F 88 8
Frome to Bristol B 77 0
G
Galashiels to Edinburgh F 52 9
Gloucester to Bristol D 35 7
Gloucester to Cardiff D 66 1
Gosport - Branch Lines around A 36 9
Greece Narrow Gauge D 72 2
H
Hampshire Narrow Gauge D 36 4
Harrow to Watford D 14 2
Harwich & Hadleigh - BLs to F 02 4
Harz Revisited F 62 8
Hastings to Ashford A 37 6
Hawick to Galashiels F 36 9
Hawkhurst - Branch Line to A 66 6
Hayling - Branch Line to A 12 3
Hay-on-Wye - BL around D 92 0
Haywards Heath to Seaford A 28 4
Hemel Hempstead - BLs to D 88 3
Henley, Windsor & Marlow - BLa C77 2
Hereford to Newport D 54 8
Hertford & Hatfield - BLs a E 58 1
Hertford Loop E 71 0
Hexham to Carlisle D 75 3
Hexham to Hawick F 08 6
Hitchin to Peterborough D 07 4
Holborn Viaduct to Lewisham A 81 9
Horsham - Branch Lines to A 02 4
Huntingdon - Branch Line to A 93 2
I
Ilford to Shenfield C 97 0
Ilfracombe - Branch Line to B 21 3
Industrial Rlys of the South East A 09 3
Ipswich to Diss F 81 9
Ipswich to Saxmundham C 41 3
Isle of Man Railway Journey G 02 9
Isle of Wight Lines - 50 yrs C 12 3
Italy Narrow Gauge F 17 8
K
Kent Narrow Gauge C 45 1
Kettering to Nottingham F 82-6
Kidderminster to Shrewsbury E 10 9
Kingsbridge - Branch Line to C 98 7
Kings Cross to Potters Bar E 62 8
King's Lynn to Hunstanton F 58 1
Kingston & Hounslow Loops A 83 3
Kingswear - Branch Line to C 17 8
L
Lambourn - Branch Line to C 70 3
Launceston & Princetown - BLs C 19 2
Leek - Branch Line From G 01 2
Leicester to Burton F 85 7
Lewisham to Dartford A 92 5
Lincoln to Cleethorpes F 56 7
Lincoln to Doncaster G 03 6
Lines around Stamford F 98 7
Lines around Wimbledon B 75 6
Liverpool Street to Chingford D 01 2
Liverpool Street to Ilford C 34 5
Llandeilo to Swansea E 46 8
London Bridge to Addiscombe B 20 6
London Bridge to East Croydon A 58 1
Longmoor - Branch Lines to A 41 3
Looe - Branch Line to C 22 2
Loughborough to Nottingham F 68 0
Lowestoft - BLs around E 40 6
Ludlow to Hereford E 14 7
Lydney - Branch Lines around E 26 0
Lyme Regis - Branch Line to A 45 1
Lynton - Branch Line to B 04 6
M
Machynlleth to Barmouth E 54 3
Maesteg and Tondu Lines E 06 2
Majorca & Corsica Narrow Gauge F 41 3
March - Branch Lines around B 09 1
Market Drayton - BLs around F 67 3
Market Harborough to Newark F 86 4
Marylebone to Rickmansworth D 49 4
Melton Constable to Yarmouth Bch E031
Midhurst - Branch Lines of E 78 9
Midhurst - Branch Lines to F 00 0
Minehead - Branch Line to A 80 2
Mitcham Junction Lines B 01 5
Monmouth - Branch Lines to E 20 8
Monmouthshire Eastern Valleys D 71 5
Moretonhampstead - BL to C 27 7
Moreton-in-Marsh to Worcester D 26 5
Morpeth to Bellingham F 87 1
Mountain Ash to Neath D 80 7
N
Newark to Doncaster F 78 9
Newbury to Westbury C 66 6
Newcastle to Hexham D 69 2
Newport (IOW) - Branch Lines to A 26 0
Newquay - Branch Lines to C 71 0
Newton Abbot to Plymouth C 60 4
Newtown to Aberystwyth E 41 3
Northampton to Peterborough F 92 5
North East German NG D 44 9
Northern Alpine Narrow Gauge F 37 6
Northern France Narrow Gauge C 75 8
Northern Spain Narrow Gauge E 83 3
North London Line B 94 7
North of Birmingham F 55 0
North Woolwich - BLs around C 65 9
Nottingham to Boston F 70 3
Nottingham to Lincoln F 43 7
O
Ongar - Branch Line to E 05 5
Orpington to Tonbridge B 03 9
Oswestry - Branch Lines around E 60 4
Oswestry to Whitchurch E 81 9
Oxford to Bletchley D 57 9
Oxford to Moreton-in-Marsh D 15 9
P
Paddington to Ealing C 37 6
Paddington to Princes Risborough C819
Padstow - Branch Line to B 54 1
Pembroke and Cardigan - BLs to F 29 1
Peterborough to Kings Lynn E 32 1
Peterborough to Lincoln F 89 5
Peterborough to Newark F 72 7
Plymouth - BLs around B 98 5
Plymouth to St. Austell C 63 5
Pontypool to Mountain Ash D 65 4
Pontypridd to Merthyr F 14 7
Pontypridd to Port Talbot E 86 4
Porthmadog 1954-94 - BLa B 31 2
Portmadoc 1923-46 - BLa B 13 8
Portsmouth to Southampton A 31 4
Portugal Narrow Gauge E 67 3
Potters Bar to Cambridge D 70 8
Princes Risborough - BL to D 05 0
Princes Risborough to Banbury C 85 7
R
Railways to Victory C 16 1
Reading to Basingstoke B 27 5
Reading to Didcot C 79 6
Reading to Guildford A 47 5
Redhill to Ashford A 73 4
Return to Blaenau 1970-82 C 64 2
Rhyl to Bangor F 15 4
Rhymney & New Tredegar Lines E 48 2
Rickmansworth to Aylesbury D 61 6
Romania & Bulgaria NG E 23 9
Romneyrail C 32 1
Ross-on-Wye - BLs around E 30 7
Ruabon to Barmouth E 84 0
Rugby to Birmingham E 37 6
Rugby to Loughborough F 12 3
Rugby to Stafford F 07 9
Rugeley to Stoke-on-Trent F 90 1
Ryde to Ventnor A 19 2
S
Salisbury to Westbury B 39 8
Sardinia and Sicily Narrow Gauge F 50 5
Saxmundham to Yarmouth C 69 7
Saxony & Baltic Germany Revisited F 71 0
Saxony Narrow Gauge D 47 0
Seaton & Sidmouth - BLs to A 95 6
Selsey - Branch Line to A 04 8
Sheerness - Branch Line to B 16 2
Shenfield to Ipswich E 96 3
Shrewsbury - Branch Line to A 86 4
Shrewsbury to Chester E 70 3
Shrewsbury to Crewe F 48 2
Shrewsbury to Ludlow E 21 5
Shrewsbury to Newtown E 29 1
Sierra Leone Narrow Gauge D 28 9
Sirhowy Valley Line E 12 3
Sittingbourne to Ramsgate A 90 1
Skegness & Mablethorpe - BL to F 84 0
Slough to Newbury C 56 7
South African Two-foot gauge E 51 2
Southampton to Bournemouth A 42 0
Southend & Southminster BLs E 76 5
Southern Alpine Narrow Gauge F 22 2
Southern France Narrow Gauge C 47 5
South London Line B 46 6
South Lynn to Norwich City F 03 1
Southwold - Branch Line to A 15 4
Spalding - Branch Lines around E 52 9
Spalding to Grimsby F 65 9 6
Stafford to Chester F 34 5
Stafford to Wellington F 59 8
St Albans to Bedford D 08 1
St. Austell to Penzance C 67 3
St. Boswell to Berwick F 44 4
Steaming Through Isle of Wight A
Steaming Through West Hants A
Stourbridge to Wolverhampton E
St. Pancras to Barking D 68 5
St. Pancras to Folkestone E 88 8
St. Pancras to St. Albans C 78 9
Stratford to Cheshunt F 53 6
Stratford-u-Avon to Birmingham D
Stratford-u-Avon to Cheltenham C
Sudbury - Branch Lines to F 19 2
Surrey Narrow Gauge C 87 1
Sussex Narrow Gauge C 68 0
Swaffham - Branch Lines around F
Swanage to 1999 - BL to A 33 8
Swanley to Ashford B 45 9
Swansea - Branch Lines around F
Swansea to Carmarthen E 59 8
Swindon to Bristol C 96 3
Swindon to Gloucester D 46 3
Swindon to Newport D 30 2
Swiss Narrow Gauge C 94 9
T
Talyllyn 60 E 98 7
Tamworth to Derby F 76 5
Taunton to Barnstaple B 60 2
Taunton to Exeter C 82 6
Taunton to Minehead F 39 0
Tavistock to Plymouth B 88 6
Tenterden - Branch Line to A 21 5
Three Bridges to Brighton A 35 2
Tilbury Loop C 86 4
Tiverton - BLs around C 62 8
Tivetshall to Beccles D 41 8
Tonbridge to Hastings A 44 4
Torrington - Branch Lines to B 37 4
Tourist Railways of France G 04 3
Towcester - BLs around E 39 0
Tunbridge Wells BLs A 32 1
U
Upwell - Branch Line to B 64 0
Uttoxeter to Macclesfield G 05 0
V
Victoria to Bromley South A 98 7
Victoria to East Croydon A 40 6
Vivarais Revisited E 08 6
W
Walsall Routes F 45 1
Wantage - Branch Line to D 25 8
Wareham to Swanage 50 yrs D098
Waterloo to Windsor A 54 3
Waterloo to Woking A 38 3
Watford to Leighton Buzzard D 45 6
Wellingborough to Leicester F 73 4
Welshpool to Llanfair E 49 9
Wenford Bridge to Fowey C 09 3
Westbury to Bath B 55 3
Westbury to Taunton C 76 5
West Cornwall Mineral Rlys D 48 7
West Croydon to Epsom B 08 4
West German Narrow Gauge D 93 7
West London - BLs of C 50 5
West London Line B 84 8
West Wiltshire - BLs of D 12 8
Weymouth - BLs A 65 9
Willesden Jn to Richmond B 71 8
Wimbledon to Beckenham C 58 1
Wimbledon to Epsom B 62 6
Wimborne - BLs around A 97 0
Wisbech - BLs around C 01 7
Witham & Kelvedon - BLs a E 82 6
Woking to Alton A 59 8
Woking to Portsmouth A 25 3
Woking to Southampton A 55 0
Wolverhampton to Shrewsbury E444
Wolverhampton to Stafford F 79 6
Worcester to Birmingham D 97 5
Worcester to Hereford D 38 8
Worthing to Chichester A 06 2
Wrexham to New Brighton F 47 5
Wroxham - BLs around F 31 4
Y
Yeovil - 50 yrs change C 38 3
Yeovil to Dorchester A 76 5
Yeovil to Exeter A 91 8
York to Scarborough F 23 9